ADDITIONAL PRAISE FOR *WELL SEASONED*

"Mary's personality shines through this work to transform how we view cooking for ourselves and our friends and family. She makes world-class meals achievable at home with this collection of approachable recipes for any occasion or season."

Arlene Dickinson

Beloved home cook, television star, and bestselling author Mary Berg is back with 100 seasonal recipes to inspire your year and delight your palate.

For Mary, cooking meals to enjoy with family is a constant source of joy, no matter the day or time of year. But as for what those meals include? Well, that's what makes it fun. As the seasons change, so does the food Mary craves and cooks. Sometimes it's based on what's available at the farmers' market, other times it's based on the weather or how she feels on a particular day. *Well Seasoned* is a cookbook to celebrate friends and family, giving readers a peek into how Mary cooks over the course of a year.

Spring is Crisp, Light, and Lively, with Green Risotto, White Wine Coq au Vin, and Pistachio Sponge Cakes with Matcha Cream

Summer is Bright, Fresh, and Classic, with Cottage Pancakes, Grilled Summer Squash Pizza, and Neapolitan Ice Cream Cake

Autumn is Cozy, Hearty, and Nostalgic, with Baked Meatballs with Pesto and Ricotta, Curried Shrimp Orzo, and Pumpkin Pecan Pudding

Winter is Rich, Savory, and Celebratory, with Everything Bagel Drop Biscuits, Roasted Fennel and Beet Salad, and Eggnog Basque Cheesecake

The recipes in this book range from easy weeknight meals to more elaborate weekend feasts, but all of them share Mary's simple instructions and warm style. With Mary's guidance and encouragement, you'll find beautiful recipes to nourish yourself and your family all year long.

Well Seasoned

A YEAR'S WORTH OF
DELICIOUS RECIPES

Mary Berg

appetite
by RANDOM HOUSE

Appetite by Random House® and colophon are registered trademarks of Penguin Random House LLC.

Library and Archives of Canada Cataloguing in Publication is available upon request.

ISBN: 9780147531261
eBook ISBN: 9780147531278

Cover and book design by Talia Abramson and Jennifer Griffiths
Photography by Lauren Vandenbrook
Art direction by Jenna Mariash

Printed in China

Published in Canada by Appetite by Random House®,
a division of Penguin Random House LLC.

www.penguinrandomhouse.ca

10 9 8 7 6 5 4 3 2 1

appetite
by RANDOM HOUSE | Penguin
Random House
Canada

For my dad,
the original cook of the house

Introduction

I think the best way to describe my relationship with food is as a forever love affair.

Ever since I can remember, it has been my constant companion, and I don't think a waking hour has passed without me daydreaming about all of the different foods I could buy, invent, cook, and eat. I'm sure this love is requited, as food has always been there to satiate any craving I've had or manage any mood I might find myself in, but I am under no illusion that it is exclusive.

In fact, my hope is that most people have this "forever love" relationship with food, one that is based on sustenance and nourishment as much as it is on comfort and enjoyment. As my favorite cartoon rat once said with respect to us humans,

"There's something about them. They don't just survive, they discover, they create. I mean, just look at what they do with food!" —Remy, *Ratatouille*

Food is something to be relished and should feed not only your body but also your soul. For me, there is pure excitement in tasting the first basket of juicy sun-warmed strawberries brought home from the farmers' market, or in smelling the grill during a backyard barbecue on a hot summer day. I feel so at ease when I sit in front of a meal that transports me back to childhood, or when I breathe in the warmth of a steaming bowl of hearty stew or a holiday feast as snow starts to cover the ground. In my life, food has always satisfied something so much bigger than hunger, and I always try to capture that momentous effect in my kitchen and in my recipes.

For those who joined me in my celebration of kitchen parties with my last book, *Kitchen Party: Effortless Recipes for Every Occasion*, you'll know that the recipes focused on cooking for crowds and making any meal into a celebration of friends and family. I wanted to make a guidebook for people who felt nervous inviting others into their homes and to quash any thoughts that a kitchen party should be anything like dining at a restaurant. While those recipes could all be halved to serve your family any night of the week, they were developed with gatherings in mind, and both the actual recipes and their yields reflected that.

Don't get me wrong. The recipes you'll find in these pages will make for some amazing kitchen parties as well, but I wanted this book to be a little more personal. *Well Seasoned* is still all about food, friends, and family, because cooking and eating are all about sharing and showing love. But in this book, the recipes are inspired by how my family and I eat every day.

As the seasons change, so does the food I crave and cook. Sometimes I cook based on what's available at the farmers' market, other times it's based on the weather, and sometimes it's based on how I feel on a particular day. *Well Seasoned* is a true peek into my kitchen and what you can expect to find gracing my table any time of year.

As with all of my recipes, all the ingredients mentioned in this book can be easily found at an average grocery store or farmers' market or even in your own pantry. I've used basic kitchen equipment, because there is nothing I dislike more than finding a recipe that I want to make, only to realize I don't have the tools to do so. As I hope you've come to expect from me, this book is filled with recipes that not only are cookable but will make you look like the absolute culinary wizard I know you are.

Welcome to my kitchen, where seasons, mood, and cravings come together into a year's worth of all things delicious.

Mary xoox

Mary

Seasonal-ish

As the seasons pass throughout the year, there are a few key themes that ebb and flow in my kitchen—that's why the best way I can describe how I cook and eat is seasonal-ish.

While a true seasonal cookbook is governed by the availability of ingredients, with certain recipes only possible during those few weeks that a key component can be found at a local farmers' market, this book is more about what I crave and when.

Like so many of us, I eat how I feel, and there is a certain rhythm I naturally follow as the year goes by.

Starting with the season of new beginnings, spring brings fresh air and light into my home. After the dark and cold of winter, sweet spring mornings are drenched in the glow of a slow sunrise and afternoons seem to creep into evenings, causing dinnertime to inch a little later with every passing day. Citrus season is still in full swing, maple syrup is being refined, and farmers' markets are popping up, with fruits and vegetables becoming more beautiful and bountiful by the week.

In the spring, I crave crisp flavors, lighter and livelier than those I found comfort in during the winter. Quick-cooking proteins like fish, shellfish, and eggs shine beside zingy and flavorful sides. Sweets are a bit dainty, fruity, and often a little nutty, a small carry-over from the rich and unctuous desserts of winter.

As balmy mornings and afternoons stretch to their limit, almost skipping evening entirely and hopping straight into starry nights, summer has me dreaming of family trips and vacations. My taste buds and temperament drift toward vibrant colors, bold flavors, and recipes that are perfect for casual get-togethers, outdoor dining, and weekends at the cottage. The variety of ingredients available at markets and shops is a treasure trove of all things delicious, and I never want to miss a single bite.

In the summer, my table is laid with classic cottage breakfasts and bakery-inspired treats, craveable crispy snacks, everything and anything that can be cooked on the grill, and meals that have me in and out of the kitchen in a flash so as to not miss out on any of the fun. Desserts are chilled, creamy, and a little fruity, with a nod to my childhood summertime faves.

As nights cool down and the leaves begin to change, the feeling of nostalgia starts to take root in my cooking. While the transition from summer to autumn impacts my life less than it did when I was a kid heading back into the classroom, autumn continues to provide a marked swing in my mood and my day-to-day activities. Perhaps it's the crunchy leaves underfoot, the smell of afternoon bonfires, or the need to throw on an extra sweater, but autumn tends to turn me into a wistful homebody.

Along with the leaves and the light in the sky, my cooking turns decidedly golden brown and my cravings call back to the things that I have always loved to eat. Classic brown-bag flavor combinations like PB&J and anything sandwich-able are frequently invoked, breakfast through dinner gets increasingly savory and hearty, and the sweets I most want are the ones that remind me of what my mom used to make or buy for afternoon snacks.

When the first quiet snowfall knocks, hinting at brazen blizzards to come, the close-knit feeling of autumn continues, and casual dinner party invitations start to go out. The short days and long nights of winter are perfect for slow, lingering meals shared between the closest of friends.

My winter appetite brings dishes both sweet and savory to the table with a not-unsubstantial focus on two of my favorite ingredient categories: starch and dairy. Bready biscuits and buns, succulent slow-cooked mains, holiday classics, potatoes galore, and satisfying sweets are the name of the game when the chill of winter rolls around, holidays in tow. Rich, bold, and warm, winter is the time to stay in and celebrate family and friends over a good home-cooked meal.

Within each season, I've divided the recipes into two general sections: Breakfast through Dinner is where you'll find all of the mains. Snacks, Sides, Sweets, and Sips is where nibbles, appetizers, side dishes, desserts, and drinks live.

The seasonality in this book is by no means prescriptive. I've cooked meals from summer in the dead of winter and autumn favorites all spring long. Who's to say when a mood or a craving may strike, and just because a certain season makes *me* feel a certain way, it doesn't mean that rings true for you. As always, if you simply cook with love and aim to nourish the stomachs and souls of the people in your life, you'll be golden.

Ingredients, Equipment, and Everyday Tips

Here is a glimpse into my kitchen that highlights the staple ingredients I love, my most-used kitchen tools, and a few everyday tips and tricks I've picked up along the way that help keep me cooking all year round.

Ingredients

DAIRY

Probably my favorite ingredient category, dairy brings richness, creaminess, and body to recipes ranging from sweet to savory, breakfast to dessert. All the recipes in this book use full-fat versions for cheese, cream cheese, sour cream, and yogurt, as these are what work best in both baking and cooking and are what I prefer to eat. For milk, all recipes were tested with whole, though 2% can be used if that is what you keep in your fridge. When using buttermilk, shake well before adding to a recipe. If you don't have buttermilk on hand, you can swap in milk mixed with a small amount of acid (such as white vinegar, cider vinegar, or lemon juice). Mix at a ratio of 1 cup of milk to 1 tablespoon of acid, then measure out the amount called for in the recipe. This mixture won't be as thick as commercial buttermilk but it will work well in a pinch. When a recipe calls for cream, the type and fat percentage is indicated.

In most baking recipes, butter and cream cheese are at room temperature, as are eggs for optimal baking results. At the risk of being redundant, the temperature of both butter and cream cheese is specified in recipes where temperature is integral for success.

FATS

With respect to butter, I always have both salted and unsalted on hand. Salted butter is what I refer to as "table butter," as it's what I spread onto muffins, toast, and rolls. For all cooking purposes, unsalted is the way to go, as it allows you to control the amount of salt that goes into a recipe and will not impact the end result. I feel very Ina saying this, but if you can, use good-quality butter, whether it is European-style (that

is, higher in fat), cultured, and/or grass-fed. Your taste buds will thank you for it.

For oils, my pantry staples are canola oil (though any neutral-flavored oil would make a perfect substitute), a cooking olive oil that won't break the bank, and a fancy finishing extra virgin olive oil with a peppery kick for dishes where the oil is not heated.

MEAT AND FISH

To ensure you are purchasing ethically raised protein from a reputable source, I suggest getting to know your local butcher and fishmonger. They are an indispensable source of information about the quality and origin of the proteins we buy.

I do not eat poultry, beef, pork, or lamb, but I do prepare it, and I find that knowing the person doing the butchering and the farm where it was raised makes for a more careful and thoughtful cook.

PRODUCE

It should come as no surprise that, being a fan of seasonal-ish cooking, I love farmers' markets and those little side-of-the-road fruit and vegetable stands. When available, these are my first choice for farm-fresh ingredients, but the certainty that a grocery store provides also makes that a good choice. In terms of grocery stores, I don't necessarily shop at the most expensive ones—rather, I look for stores that have a good number of shoppers and a high turnover of fruits and veg, which ensures that what I'm getting is fresh.

My main trick when it comes to picking the perfect fruits and vegetables (other than asking the grower at a market) has everything to do with my senses. With fruits, the trick is to use your nose. If that strawberry smells like a strawberry, you can count on it to taste like one too. With vegetables, it's mainly a looks game. Look for bright colors and freshness but don't be scared away by a few blemishes. That's just nature, baby!

To maintain the zippy flavor of citrus fruits, all citrus juices used in the recipes are freshly squeezed.

SEASONING, SPICES, AND SALTS

In my kitchen, and in every recipe I make, black pepper is always freshly ground, as the stuff you find in the shaker tends to taste dusty rather than spicy and smoky. If you can't remember the last time you bought a certain spice, especially a pre-ground one, it's probably time to think about replacing it. While old spices won't ruin a recipe, they do

start to lose their flavor after about six months. In these recipes, all herbs are fresh unless otherwise specified.

I'm sure you've heard it a hundred times before, but salt is truly the most important ingredient in a cook's cupboard. It wicks out unwanted moisture from uncooked proteins and vegetables, makes everything somehow taste like a better version of itself, and creates a necessary foil to sugar in all things sweet. My favorite everyday salt is kosher, Diamond Crystal brand to be exact. It has a nicely sized flake and is not as sharp as other varieties of salt. You'll see in this book that I use kosher salt in both savory and sweet recipes. I find that, once blended and baked in, there is little to no difference, so I don't bother with another everyday salt.

In addition to that, I have about half a dozen fun finishing salts in my pantry. No two get more use than smoked Maldon sea salt, for its subtle smoky flavor, and my favorite flaky sea salt from Newfoundland Salt Company. The crispy crystals give my dishes a true taste of Canada's east coast, and what could be better than that?

BOOZY STUFF

When cooking with wine, beer, or spirits, always go with a tried-and-true pick. You know, something you keep around the house to have on a Tuesday for no reason at all. Don't use the fancy stuff you're saving for company or for a special occasion, just use something that tastes good to you.

Equipment

BLADES

My super-sharp 8-inch chef's knife is the unsung hero of my kitchen. I have a whole row of perfectly good knives at my disposal, but this little baby is what I reach for 99.9% of the time, as it's the perfect tool for prepping, carving, slicing, and serving. A chef's knife and a good set of kitchen shears are all you need in terms of handheld blades to make every single recipe in this book.

For sharp gadgets, I like to keep things minimal. A standard food processor and either an immersion or stand blender are indispensable tools in my kitchen and will help make quick work of chopping, blending, and pureeing.

BOARDS

To go with my knife, I consider one large wood and one large plastic cutting board to be investment pieces. Not only will the size make prep much easier but the materials will help keep the edge of your knife sharp and straight, making visits to the knife sharpener less frequent.

COOKWARE AND BAKEWARE

Many recipes in this book call for a large Dutch oven. A French oven is a great alternative, but if you have neither, a large all-metal pot covered tightly with aluminum foil will do the trick. No matter the vessel, a 5- to 6-quart capacity is the perfect all-purpose size that isn't too heavy and is easy to store.

Large rimmed baking sheets are used pretty much daily in my house. For baking, they get lined with parchment paper, another staple in my kitchen. A few recipes call for specialty pans such as a removable-bottom tart pan, a springform pan, and a removable-bottom tube pan. If you like to bake, these are all good additions to your pan arsenal and can be used for lots of other recipes.

Finally, I am obsessed with my stand mixer. I use it at least five times a week, but if, unlike me, you are not that into baking or just don't have room on your counter, a hand mixer will work for any recipe that requires whipping, beating, and creaming. Recipes that will work by hand, like bread dough, include manual instructions.

Everyday Tips and Tricks

LAST-MINUTE ADDITIONS

When you're giving your dish a final taste just before serving, ask yourself if it's a little dull, a little flat, or just missing something. For dullness, add a small splash of acid like lemon juice or vinegar. For flat or less-than-flavorful food, a little more kosher salt or even some finishing salt should help. If there's something missing that I can't quite put my finger on, I find that a bit of butter or a drizzle of extra virgin olive oil can make a world of difference. These last little tweaks can help awaken your taste buds and bring a dish from okay to great.

RANDOM POINTERS

Over the years, I've learned that there are a few things I do in my kitchen that save me lots of time and headaches. I thought I should share these with you.

First, wrap your fresh ginger in plastic wrap, then freeze it as soon as you bring it home from the grocery store. This helps keep it fresh for months, removes the need to peel it before using as the freezing process softens the skin up, and makes it incredibly easy to grate into any recipe that requires it.

Second, if a recipe calls for minced garlic, just grate it using a rasp or Microplane. If there is one kitchen task I hate, it is mincing garlic on a cutting board. It's annoying, it's finicky, and I have yet to figure out how to quickly get rid of that garlicky smell.

Third, when searing meat, make sure you dry off the outside as much as possible with paper towel. If you don't do this step, steam could form between the meat and the pan and that would prevent a delicious, golden-brown sear.

Fourth, for the best baking results, make sure your ingredients are at room temperature unless otherwise specified. This will allow the ingredients to come together faster and more evenly. Also, when greasing pans for cakes and cookies, nonstick cooking spray is the best option, but wiping them down with paper towel and a little canola or neutral oil will also work. Avoid using butter unless you are also flouring the pan as the milk solids and lactose sugars can burn and crystalize, making your cookies and cakes difficult to remove.

Finally, get to know your oven. For instance, the back left corner of my oven has a hot spot, so I know to rotate pans or, if possible, avoid that corner for foods that brown easily. To figure out if your oven has any hot spots, and if so, where they are, I suggest making a batch of sugar cookies or Linzer Cookies (page 238) and baking them without rotating. Any uneven color on the cookies will indicate where your oven runs hot or cool. Knowing your oven is the best way to ensure success in all of your kitchen escapades.

Spring

Crisp, Light, and Lively

Swirled Almond Croissant Loaf

BREAKFAST THROUGH DINNER · MAKES 1 LARGE LOAF

FOR THE DOUGH

3½–4 cups bread flour

1 tablespoon sugar

2 teaspoons instant yeast

1½ teaspoons kosher salt

½ cup milk, warmed

¼ cup maple syrup

3 tablespoons canola oil

1 egg

FOR THE FILLING

¼ cup butter, room temperature

¼ cup sugar

1 egg

1 egg white

2 teaspoons almond extract

1 teaspoon vanilla extract

1½ cups almond flour

1 cup icing sugar

⅓ cup all-purpose flour

½ teaspoon kosher salt

FOR THE TOPPING

1 egg yolk

1 tablespoon milk

1 tablespoon turbinado sugar

¼ cup slivered almonds

When I first started dreaming of this book baby, I had lofty plans of concocting a recipe for easy croissants. After spending the better part of a month testing and re-testing shortcuts, I realized that the term "easy croissant" is about as big of an oxymoron as "jumbo shrimp." But this stunner of a loaf has all the sweet, frangipane-y goodness of an almond croissant with, in my opinion, even more drama than its flaky counterpart.

For the dough, in a mixing bowl, or a stand mixer fitted with a dough hook attachment, combine 3½ cups of the flour with the sugar, yeast, and salt. Make a well in the center and add ¾ cup warm tap water along with the warmed milk, maple syrup, oil, and egg. Mix it all into a shaggy dough, then knead on medium-low speed until a smooth, springy ball of dough forms, about 4 to 5 minutes, adding more flour if the dough is sticky.

Form the dough into a ball and transfer it to a lightly greased bowl. Cover with plastic wrap or a dinner plate and let the dough rise in a warm spot until doubled in bulk, 1½ to 2 hours.

Meanwhile, make the filling by beating the butter and sugar in a mixing bowl, or a stand mixer fitted with a paddle attachment, on high speed until well combined. Add the egg, egg white, and both extracts and beat to combine. In a separate bowl, stir together the almond flour, icing sugar, all-purpose flour, and salt. Add the dry ingredients to the butter mixture and mix on low to combine.

When the dough has risen, punch it down, give yourself a thumbs-up, then turn it out onto a lightly floured work surface. Roll the dough into a rectangle, about 15 × 18 inches, and evenly spread the filling on top, going right to the edges. Starting at one of the longer edges, roll the dough tightly into a log and pinch the seam shut. Using a sharp knife and starting about 1 inch from one end of the log, cut down the length of the log so you have two halves attached at one end.

With the exposed filling edge of each side of the log facing up, twist the two sides together by carefully lifting one side over the other like you would a braid. Spiral the twist into a round loaf around the uncut end

of the dough, keeping the filling edge facing up, then transfer to a large piece of parchment paper. Place the parchment and dough in an 8- or 9-inch round baking pan, cover it with a mixing bowl, and allow it to rise for 1 to 1½ hours until puffy and almost doubled in size.

Preheat your oven to 375°F.

Make the topping by beating together the egg yolk and milk. Brush this over the top of the unbaked loaf and scatter the sugar then the almonds over top. Bake the loaf for 40 to 45 minutes until golden brown and hollow-sounding when tapped, or the internal temperature reaches between 190°F and 200°F. If the loaf is becoming too brown while baking, place a loose tent of aluminum foil over it while it continues to bake. Allow the loaf to cool in the pan for 20 minutes before lifting it out onto a wire rack to cool completely. Cover the loaf and store at room temperature for up to 5 days.

One Giant Hot Cross Bun

BREAKFAST THROUGH DINNER · MAKES 1 GIANT BUN

¼ cup apple juice

¼ cup finely diced dried apricots

¼ cup chopped dried cranberries

¼ cup dried currants

¼ cup golden raisins

3½–4 cups + ¼ cup all-purpose flour, divided

¼ cup packed brown sugar

2 teaspoons instant yeast

1¾ teaspoons kosher salt

1 teaspoon ground cinnamon

¼ teaspoon ground cloves

¼ teaspoon ground nutmeg

1 cup milk, warmed

¼ cup butter, melted

2 eggs, lightly beaten

1 tablespoon orange zest

1 teaspoon vanilla extract

1 egg yolk

1 cup icing sugar

3 tablespoons orange juice (about ½ orange)

Hot cross buns were a Good Friday staple at my church when I was growing up, but I always hated the sickly sweet, syrupy, glacé fruit studded throughout store-bought ones and gravitated to the plate of broken Chips Ahoy! cookies instead. For this giant hot cross bun, glacé fruit can get right on out of here, because plumped-up dried apricots, cranberries, currants, and golden raisins are here to stay. This is best enjoyed fresh with butter, and maybe a sprinkling of cinnamon sugar, but any leftovers make for some amazing French toast or bread pudding.

Line a large baking sheet with parchment paper and set aside.

In a small microwave-safe dish, stir together the apple juice, apricots, cranberries, currants, and raisins. Microwave on high for 30 seconds or until warm. Set aside to cool to room temperature.

In a mixing bowl, or a stand mixer fitted with a dough hook attachment, mix 3½ cups of the flour with the sugar, yeast, salt, cinnamon, cloves, and nutmeg on low speed to combine. Pour in the warmed milk, melted butter, eggs, zest, vanilla, and cooled fruit mixture. Knead on medium-low speed until a soft, springy dough forms, about 5 to 6 minutes, adding more flour if the dough is sticky.

When the dough has come together, transfer it to a lightly greased bowl. Cover with plastic wrap or a dinner plate, and let the dough rise in a warm spot until doubled in bulk, about 1½ hours.

When the dough has risen, punch it down and turn it out onto a lightly floured work surface. Shape it into a tight-skinned ball by folding the edges into the center until the underside looks smooth and tight. Flip the ball seam-side down and place it on the prepared baking sheet. Lightly drape the dough with a clean kitchen towel and allow it to rise for another hour or until almost doubled in size.

Preheat your oven to 375°F. Set a wire rack on a parchment-lined baking sheet.

In a small bowl, combine the remaining ¼ cup of flour with 3 table-spoons of water. Transfer this to a piping bag fitted with a plain tip or to a resealable plastic bag with one corner cut off. In a separate bowl, make an egg wash by whisking the egg yolk with 1 tablespoon of water.

Brush the loaf with the egg wash. Using the piping bag, pipe a line down the center of the loaf and repeat in the other direction to create a cross.

Bake the loaf for 35 to 40 minutes until golden brown and hollow-sounding when tapped or the internal temperature is between 190°F and 200°F. Remove from the oven and transfer to the wire rack. In a bowl, whisk together the icing sugar and orange juice to make a glaze and pour it over the still-warm loaf.

Enjoy warm, with an optional swipe of butter and a bit of cinnamon, or, if you're feeling fancy, Maple Orange Butter (page 190). Cover and store the loaf at room temperature for up to 5 days.

Maple Sesame Almond Butter

BREAKFAST THROUGH DINNER · MAKES ABOUT 1¾ CUPS

2½ cups raw almonds

2 tablespoons white sesame seeds

¼ cup pure maple syrup

1 tablespoon melted coconut oil, plus more if needed

½ teaspoon kosher salt

To my mind, there is no truer sign of spring's arrival than the sight of steel pails tacked onto the sides of maple trees lining country roads and wooded paths. As soon as freezing temperatures break, the maple sap starts to pour, and that means it's almost time for one of my very favorite ingredients, maple syrup, which also happens to be the perfect sweetener for this sesame almond butter. So good on crackers or toast, smashed into vanilla ice cream, or just eaten off a spoon, it's the perfect update to a classic spread.

Preheat your oven to 350°F and line a baking sheet with parchment paper.

In a mixing bowl, stir together the almonds, sesame seeds, maple syrup, and melted coconut oil until well combined. Transfer to the prepared baking sheet and bake until the almonds smell nutty and the maple syrup is a little tacky, 12 to 14 minutes. Remove from the oven and allow the mixture to cool completely.

Transfer the mixture to a food processor fitted with a steel blade, scraping off any maple syrup and sesame seeds that may have stuck to the parchment. Process the mixture until creamy, 12 minutes, scraping down the sides of the bowl every few minutes.

If, after 12 minutes, the mixture is not clumping together in a sort of ball, melt another teaspoon or two of coconut oil and add it in. Continue processing until the mixture is a smooth buttery consistency, then season with salt to taste.

Store in the fridge in a jar or sealed container for up to 3 months.

Cheddar Chive Toad in a Hole

BREAKFAST THROUGH DINNER · SERVES 4

1 teaspoon olive oil

4 pork sausages, preferably bratwurst

⅔ cup all-purpose flour

½ teaspoon kosher salt

¼ teaspoon black pepper

⅔ cup milk, warmed

3 eggs

4 tablespoons finely chopped chives, divided

1 teaspoon butter

½ cup grated extra-old white cheddar

Maple syrup, for serving (optional)

I have absolutely no idea where the name "toad in a hole" comes from but I do know that this cheesy one-pan meal is a hit on my breakfast table. It's basically a savory Dutch baby with a few sausages nestled in for good measure, and it's perfect for chilly spring mornings. While it might sound a little odd with the mix of the sausage, cheese, and chives, a good glug of maple syrup is a must, if you ask me.

Place a cast iron skillet or a deep 9-inch pie plate in the center of your oven and preheat it to 425°F.

When the oven is at temperature, add the oil to the hot pan along with the sausages, return to the oven, and cook for 15 minutes.

Meanwhile, make the batter in a mixing bowl by whisking together the flour, salt, pepper, warmed milk, eggs, and 3 tablespoons of the chives until well combined, about 1 minute.

After the sausages have been cooking for 15 minutes, flip them over, add the butter to the pan, and carefully pour in the prepared batter. Return the pan to the oven and bake for 18 minutes without opening the oven door.

When the toad in a hole is extremely puffy and golden brown, scatter the cheese on top and set the oven to broil. Broil until the cheese is melted and slightly golden brown, 2 to 3 minutes. Serve immediately, scattered with the remaining chives and drizzled with maple syrup (if using).

Note:
For a vegetarian version, leave out the sausage and cook the batter in the hot skillet for 18 minutes, finishing with the cheese and a broil.

Whipped Feta Turkish Eggs

BREAKFAST THROUGH DINNER · SERVES 4 (WITH SOME LEFTOVER WHIPPED FETA)

7 oz soft feta cheese (see note)

2 tablespoons brick-style
cream cheese

1–2 garlic cloves, finely minced

1 lemon, juiced

¾ cup plain Greek yogurt

2 tablespoons butter

¼ teaspoon crushed red pepper
flakes, Marash pepper, or
Urfa Biber

2 tablespoons finely chopped
chives

2 tablespoons finely chopped
dill, plus more for serving

4–8 soft poached or fried eggs

Flaky sea salt

4 slices of bread or small,
toasted pitas

The first time I made breakfast for my mom, I brought her a breakfast-in-bed of cornflakes and water (a perpetual rule follower, I was not yet old enough to pour milk by myself, so I improvised). When I served her this dish one morning last year, the satisfied grin and a literally licked-clean plate was enough to reassure me that my skills have vastly improved since then.

Crumble the feta into a food processor fitted with a steel blade. Add the cream cheese, garlic, and lemon juice and process until well combined, scraping down the sides of the bowl as needed. Add the yogurt and blitz until creamy.

Transfer the whipped feta to a heatproof bowl and place it over a pot containing 1 inch of simmering water. Allow the feta to slowly heat, whisking occasionally.

Meanwhile, melt the butter in a small frying pan or saucepan over medium heat and cook until the butter has foamed up and golden-brown flecks appear, 5 to 8 minutes. Remove the browned butter from the heat, add the red pepper flakes, and set aside.

When the feta is warm and slightly lighter in consistency, stir in the chives and dill. Spoon the feta into four serving dishes, top with one or two poached or fried eggs, and spoon the spicy browned butter over top. Season with salt, scatter a little chopped dill over top, and serve with bread or toasted pita.

Store any leftover whipped feta in the fridge for up to 1 week.

Note:
When buying soft feta, look for cheeses that contain sheep's milk. They'll be softer and creamier, making for a smoother whipped feta.

Fine Herb and Goat Cheese French Omelet with Quick-Roasted Asparagus

BREAKFAST THROUGH DINNER · SERVES 2

1 small handful asparagus

2 teaspoons olive oil

Kosher salt and black pepper

6 eggs

2 tablespoons butter, divided

1–2 oz soft goat cheese, divided

2 teaspoons finely chopped tarragon, divided, plus more for serving

2 teaspoons finely chopped flat-leaf parsley, divided, plus more for serving

1 teaspoon finely chopped dill, divided, plus more for serving

Flaky sea salt

French omelets have always had an austere, very cheffy air about them, so, while I would order them at a snazzy bistro, I would never attempt one at home. That is, until I figured out that they're ridiculously easy and one of the fastest ways to prepare eggs. They are now my go-to breakfast, brunch, lunch, or dinner on days where I don't really want to put in the effort but still want to feel a bit ooh-là-là.

Preheat your oven to 425°F.

Trim off and discard the woody ends of the asparagus, place the asparagus on a large baking sheet, and toss with the oil. Season with salt and pepper and roast just until tender, about 10 minutes, tossing halfway through, then set aside.

In a mixing bowl, whisk the eggs with ¼ teaspoon of kosher salt until very well combined. You do not want to whisk too much air in. You just want the eggs to be a smooth consistency with no visible white or yolk remaining.

Place an 8- to 10-inch nonstick skillet over medium-low heat and add 1 tablespoon of the butter to melt. The butter should just get foamy, but do not let it sizzle. If it does sizzle, turn the heat down slightly. When the butter is melted, add half of the eggs. Holding the handle of the pan in one hand and a rubber spatula in the other, gently shake the pan while stirring the eggs.

Scrape down the sides of the skillet with the spatula and continue to shake and stir the eggs until they are a creamy curd-like consistency with not much runny liquid left. This should take about 1 to 2 minutes. At this point, shake and spread the eggs into one layer and remove the pan from the heat. Scatter half of the goat cheese down the center of the omelet, followed by half of the tarragon, parsley, and dill, and lay half of the asparagus on top of the cheese.

Allow the eggs to sit undisturbed off the heat to set the bottom, about 1 minute. Using the spatula, loosen the edges of the omelet from the skillet, then lift and roll the eggs onto themselves over the cheese and herbs. Tip the omelet from the pan and place it seam-side down on a serving plate. Cover the first omelet with an upturned mixing bowl and set aside while you make the second as you did the first.

Serve the omelets scattered with a few more finely chopped herbs and a pinch of salt.

Note:

If the omelet is not holding together after that final rest in the pan off the heat, place the pan back over medium-low heat for 30 seconds, or just until the bottom is set.

Egg Salad Tea Sandwiches with Radish Butter

BREAKFAST THROUGH DINNER · SERVES 2 TO 3

6 large eggs

2 teaspoons white vinegar

2–3 tablespoons mayonnaise

1 teaspoon grainy Dijon mustard

½ teaspoon smooth Dijon mustard

1 green onion, finely chopped

2 teaspoons finely chopped dill

1 teaspoon finely chopped flat-leaf parsley

Kosher salt and black pepper

4 radishes

3 tablespoons butter, room temperature

6 slices sandwich bread

Pea shoots (optional)

Church lady sandwiches, party sandwiches, or, as we morosely refer to them in my family, funeral sandwiches are my favorite form of tea sandwiches. Sliced into thin little rectangles, their petit dimensions somehow make them all the more delicious. While I don't hold the record in my family for the most polished off in one sitting (that belongs to my brother who, and I am not exaggerating, ate the equivalent of 14 full sandwiches), it takes all of my willpower not to greedily gobble up every last one of these perfect morsels.

To hard-boil the eggs, place them in a large saucepan, cover them in cool water, then stir in the vinegar and bring to a boil over medium heat. Cover, remove from the heat, and let sit for 13 minutes. Drain the eggs, plunge them into cold water to stop the cooking process, and peel.

Finely dice the eggs and place in a mixing bowl. Stir in 2 tablespoons of mayonnaise, both Dijons, the green onions, dill, and parsley. If desired, add another tablespoon of mayonnaise. Season with salt and pepper, cover, and refrigerate while you make the butter, or for up to 2 days.

Trim and grate the radishes onto a clean kitchen towel or a few stacked pieces of paper towel and squeeze over the sink to remove as much liquid as possible. Add the grated radishes to a bowl along with the butter, season with a good pinch of salt and some pepper, and mix well to combine.

To assemble the sandwiches, spread 3 slices of bread with the radish butter. If you're using pea shoots, lay an even layer on top of the radish butter and top with the egg salad. If you're not using pea shoots, just top the radish butter with the egg salad. Season with a little more salt and pepper, if desired, and top the sandwiches with the remaining slices of bread. Remove the crusts from the bread and cut each sandwich into three finger sandwiches.

Deviled Crab on Toast

BREAKFAST THROUGH DINNER · SERVES 2 AS A MAIN OR 6 AS AN APPETIZER

8 oz cooked crab meat

2–3 tablespoons mayonnaise

1 teaspoon Dijon mustard

1 tablespoon finely minced shallot

2 teaspoons finely chopped chives

1½ teaspoons finely chopped flat-leaf parsley

1 teaspoon finely chopped dill

½ teaspoon seafood seasoning, such as Old Bay

⅛–¼ teaspoon cayenne pepper

¼–½ lemon, juiced

Kosher salt

3 thick slices challah or brioche

3 tablespoons butter, room temperature

Sliced bread-and-butter pickles

This herby, lemony-dressed crab with just a hint of devilish heat is inspired by a dish I had at Union, one of my favorite Toronto restaurants, and it hits the spot when mounded on buttery griddled bread. The addition of bread-and-butter pickles is a true nod to Union, as they are actual wizards when it comes to sweet pickle preparation.

Place the crab meat in a fine mesh sieve and give it a press to drain any liquid it was packed in. Transfer to a large piece of paper towel and press to dry.

In a bowl, stir together 2 tablespoons of mayonnaise, the Dijon, shallots, chives, parsley, dill, seafood seasoning, ⅛ teaspoon of cayenne pepper, and the juice of ¼ lemon. Add the crab and mix until well combined, adding more mayonnaise, cayenne, and lemon juice to taste. Season the mixture with salt and refrigerate, covered, until ready to assemble or for up to 2 days.

Warm a large skillet over medium heat and lay out the bread on a work surface. If you're making this as a main, cut each piece of bread in half. If you're serving it as an appetizer, cut each piece of bread into quarters. Spread the butter over both sides of the bread and toast in the skillet until golden brown on both sides, about 2 to 3 minutes, flipping halfway through.

Top the toasted bread with the crab mixture and a few slices of bread-and-butter pickles and serve immediately.

Herby Falafel

FOR THE FALAFELS

1 cup dried chickpeas, soaked overnight (see note)

4 garlic cloves, roughly chopped

3 green onions, roughly chopped

½ cup loosely packed flat-leaf parsley

½ cup loosely packed cilantro

Zest of 1 lemon

2 teaspoons ground cumin

1 teaspoon kosher salt

¾ teaspoon ground coriander

½ teaspoon crushed red pepper flakes

4–6 tablespoons all-purpose flour

1 teaspoon baking powder

Canola oil, for frying

TO SERVE

4 pitas, Greek or pocket-style

½ cup plain Greek yogurt or Whipped Feta (page 25)

1 cup shredded lettuce or cabbage

½ cup Quick Pickled Spring Veg (page 41) (optional)

Finely diced green or red onion

1½ tablespoons tahini

3 oz feta cheese

Cilantro leaves

When my husband, Aaron, and I first started dating, we both tried to play it super chill, which is an expression that I would never use to describe myself. While on our dates I managed to play it cool, back home at my apartment you could find me frantically forcing my cell phone on my roommate, making her promise not to give it back to me until I could convince her that I wouldn't check it every 30 seconds. You know, like a real cool cat. This recipe is an homage to the fast-food falafels we would share on our first dates, walking around Waterloo Park, me absolutely crushing this whole nonchalant dating thing.

For the falafels, drain the chickpeas and place them in a food processor fitted with a steel blade. Add the garlic, green onions, parsley, cilantro, lemon zest, cumin, salt, coriander, and red pepper flakes. Pulse six to eight times, or until finely chopped and well mixed. Sprinkle 4 tablespoons of flour and the baking powder over the chickpea mixture and pulse two to three more times to combine. Test the falafel mixture by picking some up and squeezing it into a small ball with your hands. It shouldn't be too sticky and it should just hold together. If it is still sticky, add another 1 to 2 tablespoons of flour and pulse to combine.

Transfer the mixture to a bowl or resealable container, cover, and refrigerate for at least 1 hour, or up to 24 hours.

After the falafel mixture has chilled, use a large tablespoon to scoop it into walnut-sized balls. Flatten each one into a slightly squashed round, almost like a little burger patty, and place on a baking sheet.

Preheat your oven to 200°F and heat 1-inch of oil in a high-sided skillet to 375°F. If you do not have a thermometer, heat the oil until it shimmers or the end of a wooden spoon causes bubbles to form when gently dipped into it.

Fry the falafel in batches of five or six until golden brown on each side. This will take about 2 to 3 minutes per side. Transfer the cooked falafel back to the baking sheet and keep warm in the oven until ready to serve.

To serve, lay out the pitas and spread each with 2 tablespoons of yogurt. Top with shredded lettuce, falafel, pickles (if using), and onions, and a drizzle of tahini. Finally, scatter on the feta and cilantro and roll to close up the pitas.

Note:

The trick to great falafel is using dried chickpeas, not canned. To soak the chickpeas, measure out 1 cup of dried chickpeas and place them in a large bowl. Cover with at least 4 inches of water and soak for at least 12 hours, or up to 24 hours, at room temperature. Drain the water when you are ready to make the falafel.

Green Risotto

BREAKFAST THROUGH DINNER · SERVES 4 AS A MAIN OR 6 TO 8 AS A SIDE

5½ cups low-sodium vegetable broth, plus more as needed

3 tablespoons butter

4 green onions, thinly sliced

Kosher salt and black pepper

2 garlic cloves, minced

1½ cups Arborio rice

½ cup dry white wine, such as Pinot Grigio

½ cup green peas, fresh or frozen

4 large handfuls baby spinach

¼ cup chopped chives

¼ cup chopped flat-leaf parsley

1 tablespoon chopped tarragon, basil, or dill

1 lemon, zested and juiced

½ cup finely grated Pecorino Romano cheese

Risotto has always been one of my favorite recipes that allow for a vegetable crisper cleanout, but this bright and lively green risotto is a celebration of all things farmers' market fresh. With crisp peas, tender baby spinach, and so many herbs, this dish is a perfect way to revel in the season's bounty.

In a saucepan, warm the broth over low heat just until hot.

Place a large sauté pan or saucepan over medium-low heat and melt the butter. Add the green onions, season with salt and pepper, and cook, stirring frequently, until slightly translucent, about 1 to 2 minutes. Add the garlic and then the rice, turn the heat up to medium, and cook for 1 to 2 minutes, just to cook off the raw garlic and lightly toast the rice.

Stirring continuously, add the wine and cook until it's all absorbed and evaporated. Using a ladle, add about ½ cup of the hot broth into the rice and stir to combine. Stir the rice frequently until all of the broth is absorbed, then add another ½ cup. Continue adding broth in this manner until the rice is cooked to al dente. This could take anywhere from 4½ to 5 cups of broth.

When the rice is just cooked, stir in the green peas and allow them to cook just until tender, about 3 to 4 minutes.

Meanwhile, using an immersion or stand blender, purée the spinach, chives, parsley, and tarragon with the lemon zest and juice and the remaining ½ cup of broth until smooth. Season with salt and pepper. Just before serving, stir this mixture into your risotto along with the grated cheese and season with salt and pepper, adding a bit more warm broth if desired.

Sesame Beurre Blanc Pasta with Crab and Oregano

BREAKFAST THROUGH DINNER · SERVES 4

FOR THE PASTA

Kosher salt

7–9 oz dry short pasta, such as casarecce, trofie, or rotini

6 tablespoons butter

2 teaspoons toasted sesame oil

1 small shallot, finely minced

Black pepper

1 cup dry white wine, such as Pinot Grigio

¼ cup whipping (35%) cream

1 lemon, zested and juiced

1 cup finely grated Pecorino Romano cheese

8 oz cooked crab meat (see note)

FOR THE TOPPING

2 teaspoons butter

2 teaspoons toasted sesame oil

¼ cup panko breadcrumbs

2 teaspoons white sesame seeds

2 teaspoons black sesame seeds

½ teaspoon crushed red pepper flakes

2 tablespoons oregano leaves

Note:

Real crab, often found in cans or little tubs, can be a bit pricey, but it's a must for this dish. Don't substitute the real stuff with imitation.

Sometimes I find big bowls of pasta to be a little one-note after the first few bites. Don't get me wrong; there is definitely comfort in a bowl of silky stovetop mac and cheese or classic spaghetti with tomato sauce, but every now and again I crave something that keeps my taste buds on their toes. This dish does just that. Every bite is more exciting than the last, with the varying tastes and textures of the velvety butter sauce, sweet crab, crispy sesame topping, and little perfumed hits of oregano.

For the pasta, set a large pot of water to a boil over high heat and heavily season with salt. Add the pasta and cook according to the package directions, just until al dente. Reserve about 1 cup of the pasta cooking liquid, then drain the pasta and set aside.

Place a large sauté pan or skillet over medium heat and melt the butter and sesame oil. Add the shallots, season with salt and pepper, and cook just until the shallots start to turn translucent, about 2 minutes. Add the wine, bring the mixture to a simmer, and allow it to reduce by about half. This should take about 5 minutes.

When the wine mixture has reduced, mix in the cream, bring the mixture back to a simmer, and allow it to cook down a little for 2 to 3 minutes. Whisk in the lemon zest and juice, cheese, and crab meat, and turn the heat down to medium-low.

Toss the cooked pasta in the sauce, adding a few tablespoons of pasta water at a time to loosen everything and bring the sauce together. Allow the pasta and sauce to cook together slightly while you make the topping.

For the topping, in a small skillet, melt the butter and oil over medium-high heat and add the panko, both types of sesame seeds, and red pepper flakes. Stirring frequently, toast the mixture until golden brown and nutty-smelling, about 2 minutes.

Serve the pasta topped with the crunchy sesame topping and a scattering of fresh oregano leaves.

Halibut Meunière with Quick Pickled Spring Veg

BREAKFAST THROUGH DINNER · SERVES 4

FOR THE PICKLES

1 small handful asparagus

1 medium carrot

6–8 small radishes

1 small handful green peas, fresh or frozen and thawed

⅓ cup white or apple cider vinegar

2 tablespoons sugar

2 teaspoons kosher salt

1 lemon, zested and juiced

FOR THE HALIBUT

4 (each 6–7 oz) halibut fillets, skin removed

½ cup all-purpose flour

Kosher salt and black pepper

2 tablespoons canola oil

2 tablespoons + ¼ cup butter, divided

1 lemon, zested and juiced

3 tablespoons chopped flat-leaf parsley

½ lemon, cut into 4 wedges

Note:

To know when a larger fish such as halibut is done, stick a small paring knife in the center and give it a twist. The fish should flake apart a little and the knife tip should come out hot.

In cooking, the term *meunière*, or "miller" in English, simply means to dust whatever you're making in flour. It's a simple and rustic way to get a golden color on delicate proteins like fish, and it also lends itself to the quickest velvety butter pan sauce this side of the Atlantic. Here, I'm serving the fish with quick pickled spring vegetables. It's a fast and fake-fancy dish perfect for any night of the week.

For the pickles, prepare the vegetables by trimming off the woody ends of the asparagus, peeling the carrot, and trimming the tops and bottoms off the radishes. Using a vegetable peeler, peel the carrot and asparagus stalks into thin ribbons, reserving the asparagus tips for later. Using a knife, thinly slice the radishes. Place the prepared asparagus, including the tips, carrots, radishes, and peas in a small bowl and set aside.

In a small pot, combine the vinegar, sugar, and salt and bring to a simmer over medium heat just until the sugar and salt dissolve. Stir in the lemon zest and juice along with ½ cup of cool water and pour this over the prepared vegetables. Refrigerate until ready to use.

For the halibut, remove the fish from the fridge and allow it to sit at room temperature for 15 to 20 minutes. Scatter the flour into a shallow dish and pat the fish dry with paper towel. Season the fish well with salt and pepper and dredge it in the flour.

Heat a large nonstick skillet over medium-high heat. Add the oil and 2 tablespoons of butter and melt them together. When the oil and butter are hot, tap the excess flour off each fillet and place in the pan to sear until deep golden brown on the first side, about 5 minutes. Flip the fillets over and continue to cook until golden and just cooked through, 2 to 4 more minutes (see note).

Remove the halibut from the pan to rest, turn the heat down to medium, and add ¼ cup of butter. Allow the butter to cook, stirring frequently, until browned, about 2 to 3 minutes, then add the lemon zest and juice and parsley. Season with salt and pepper. Remove the sauce from the heat.

To serve, spoon the sauce over the fillets, and place the lemon wedges on the side. Remove the pickled vegetables from their liquid and serve alongside or on top of the fish.

Pistachio Pesto Salmon en Croute

BREAKFAST THROUGH DINNER · SERVES 4

½ cup loosely packed basil

¼ cup loosely packed flat-leaf parsley

¼ cup loosely packed arugula

2 tablespoons finely grated Parmigiano-Reggiano cheese

2 tablespoons shelled unsalted pistachios

1 garlic clove, peeled and smashed

½ lemon, zested and juiced

3 tablespoons olive oil

Kosher salt and black pepper

1 sheet frozen puff pastry, thawed

1½ lb salmon fillet, pin bones and skin removed

1 egg

I know a lot of people love beef Wellington, but I've always found that the bottom pastry ends up soggy and flimsy because of the juiciness of the beef tenderloin. Salmon, on the other hand, is the perfect protein to prepare in this in-pastry style. Meaty salmon stays nice and moist, while the pastry crisps up to golden perfection.

Line a baking sheet with parchment paper and set aside.

In a food processor fitted with a steel blade, prepare the pesto by combining the basil, parsley, arugula, Parmigiano-Reggiano, pistachios, garlic, lemon zest and juice, and oil. Pulse until everything is finely chopped, well mixed, and the texture of the pesto is spreadable. Taste and season with salt and pepper.

Roll out the puff pastry so it is large enough to fold over the salmon fillet. If needed, you can trim some excess pastry off one side and puzzle the pastry together so it will enclose the fillet. Spread the pesto onto one side of the pastry to make a bed for the salmon, leaving a 1-inch border around the edge. Place the fillet on top, and season with salt and pepper.

In a small bowl, beat the egg with 1 tablespoon of water to make an egg wash. Brush the outside border around the salmon with this egg wash, then refrigerate the egg wash for later use. Fold the pastry over to cover the salmon, trim the edges, and pinch to seal. Transfer the wrapped salmon onto the prepared baking sheet and refrigerate, uncovered, for at least 30 minutes, or up to 24 hours.

Position a rack at the bottom of your oven and preheat it to 425°F. Make a couple of slits in the top of the pastry with a small knife to allow steam to escape and brush the top of the pastry with the remaining egg wash. Bake just until the puff pastry is golden brown and crisp, 25 to 30 minutes. Allow the salmon en croute to rest for 5 to 10 minutes before slicing with a sharp or serrated knife and serving.

White Wine Coq au Vin

BREAKFAST THROUGH DINNER · SERVES 4 TO 6

1 chicken, broken down into drumsticks, thighs, and breasts (see note)

Kosher salt and black pepper

2 tablespoons all-purpose flour

3½ oz thick-cut bacon, diced

3 tablespoons butter, divided

1 leek, white and light green parts only, halved and sliced into ½-inch pieces

1 yellow onion, peeled and cut into 12 wedges

3 large parsnips, halved and cut diagonally into 1-inch pieces

2 large carrots, halved and cut diagonally into 1-inch pieces

3 garlic cloves, finely chopped, divided

2 tablespoons brandy

1½ cups + 2 tablespoons dry Riesling or Pinot Gris, divided

1 cup low-sodium chicken broth

8 stems flat-leaf parsley, leaves picked, chopped, and reserved

4 sprigs thyme

1 sprig sage

2 bay leaves

8 oz oyster mushrooms, roughly torn

2 tablespoons crème fraîche or sour cream

I love any recipe that calls for less than a bottle of wine. It means that I, as the cook, have every right to enjoy whatever remains in the bottle while a dish is bubbling away. Traditionally made with red wine from the Burgundy region of France, this brighter take on coq au vin is perfect for chilly spring nights.

Preheat your oven to 300°F.

Place the chicken in a large bowl, season well with salt and pepper, and sprinkle the flour over top. Toss the chicken to coat lightly with the flour and set aside.

Place a Dutch oven or braiser with a tight-fitting lid on the stove. Place the bacon in it and turn the heat on to medium. Cook until the bacon has rendered its fat and is crisp. Remove the bacon from the pot, turn the heat up to medium-high, and add 2 tablespoons of butter and the chicken, skin-side down. Sear the chicken until the skin is golden brown, about 4 to 5 minutes, then remove to a plate.

While the chicken sears, place the sliced leeks in a large bowl and cover with tap water. Run your hands through the leeks, agitating them so that any dirt falls away to the bottom of the bowl. Using your hands, scoop the leeks out of the water, allowing as much water as possible to drain away.

Once the chicken has been removed from the pan, turn the heat down to medium and add the leeks along with the onions, parsnips, and carrots. Cook, stirring frequently, just until the vegetables start to develop a little color, about 3 to 4 minutes. Add a little over half of the garlic and deglaze the pan with the brandy. Allow it to bubble away, then add 1½ cups of wine along with the broth and seared chicken.

Lay out the parsley, thyme, and sage sprigs and tie them together with a piece of butcher's twine to make a bouquet garni. Add this with the bay leaves to the pot and bring to a boil. Once boiling, cover the pot with the lid and transfer to the oven for 30 minutes.

Meanwhile, melt the remaining 1 tablespoon of butter in a sauté pan over medium-high heat and cook the mushrooms just until golden brown, about 2 to 3 minutes. Add the remaining garlic and the 2 tablespoons of wine, allow that to bubble away for 30 seconds, and remove the pan from the heat.

Transfer the stew to the stovetop, remove the lid, and place it over medium-low heat. Simmer for 15 minutes to reduce the cooking liquid. Just before serving, remove the bay leaves and bouquet garni, then stir in the mushrooms, crème fraîche, and reserved parsley. Season with salt and pepper, and serve.

Note:

If breaking down a whole chicken is not your thing, feel free to use four to six bone-in, skin-on chicken breasts, thighs, or a mix of the two.

Burrata with Salty Things

SNACKS, SIDES, SWEETS, AND SIPS · SERVES 4

1 (about 8 oz) ball burrata

4 anchovy fillets

1 cup pitted olives, green and/
or kalamata

1 small handful basil

1 small handful flat-leaf parsley

½ small handful chives

½ lemon, zested and juiced

Black pepper

2 tablespoons extra virgin
olive oil

Crackers, sliced fresh bread,
or crostini, for serving

I come from a long line of salt-loving ladies. My nana, among her many other quirks, would set a shaker down next to a cut-up apple, while my mom salts everything, from eggs to pizza, and often uses her finger to swipe up any wayward granules left on the plate. On any given day, my pantry is filled with at least half a dozen types of salt and an unknowable number of briny ingredients that can be used to bring flavorful salty kicks to pretty much anything that needs it. To the ladies in my family, this brackish burrata is a dream.

Place the burrata on a serving dish and set it out at room temperature just to take the chill of the fridge off it.

Meanwhile, place the anchovies, olives, basil, parsley, chives, and most of the lemon zest on a cutting board and chop everything together until well combined. Transfer everything to a small bowl, stir in the lemon juice, and season with pepper.

Using a knife, split open the top of the burrata to expose the creamy filling. Spoon the olive mixture over and around the burrata and drizzle with the oil. Scatter the remaining lemon zest over top. Serve with crackers, fresh bread, and/or crostini.

Sundried Tomato Chickpeas with Sweet Potato, Mint, and Feta

SNACKS, SIDES, SWEETS, AND SIPS · SERVES 4 AS A MAIN OR 6 AS A SIDE

1 sweet potato

2 teaspoons olive oil

Kosher salt and black pepper

6 oil-packed sundried tomatoes, roughly chopped

3 tablespoons sundried tomato oil

2 tablespoons tomato paste

½ lemon, zested and juiced

1 garlic clove, minced

1 tablespoon chopped flat-leaf parsley

1 tablespoon chopped mint

½ teaspoon ground cumin

¼ teaspoon smoked paprika

1 (19 oz) can chickpeas

7–8 oz feta cheese

Mint leaves, for garnish

A can of chickpeas is kind of like a kitchen Swiss army knife. You can use the chickpeas to make hummus, add them to a soup or stew for a boost of protein and fiber, or scatter them over a run-of-the-mill salad to make a quick and easy dinner. These are all great options, but sometimes I like to let the humble canned chickpea really shine. With the help of other pantry staples, a few fresh herbs, and a crumbling of feta cheese, this is one of my favorite ways to snazz up these versatile legumes.

Preheat your oven to 400°F.

Peel the sweet potato, cut it into ½-inch dice, and transfer it to a baking sheet. Drizzle the olive oil over top and season well with salt and pepper. Toss everything together and roast for 20 minutes, stirring halfway through.

Meanwhile, in a food processor fitted with a steel blade, combine the sundried tomatoes, sundried tomato oil, tomato paste, lemon zest and juice, garlic, parsley, mint, cumin, and paprika. Season with salt and pepper and pulse six to eight times to combine. The mixture should not be a smooth purée—you should still be able to see some pieces of sundried tomato and flecks of parsley and mint.

Using a rubber spatula, carefully transfer the sundried tomato mixture to a mixing bowl. Drain and rinse the chickpeas, and add them to the bowl. Add the roasted sweet potato and toss well to combine. To serve, scatter on the feta and a few mint leaves. Serve warm, at room temperature, or chilled from the fridge.

Roasted Carrots with Greeny Goodness

FOR THE ROASTED CARROTS

8–10 field carrots, peeled and stems trimmed (see note)

1 tablespoon olive oil

2 teaspoons apple cider vinegar

Kosher salt and black pepper

FOR THE GREEN SAUCE

1 cup lightly packed watercress or arugula

¼ cup lightly packed basil

2 tablespoons lightly packed flat-leaf parsley

2 tablespoons chopped chives

1 tablespoon chopped dill

1 garlic clove, roughly chopped

½ lemon, zested and juiced

¼ cup Greek yogurt or sour cream

4 tablespoons soft goat cheese, divided

1 teaspoon Dijon mustard

Kosher salt and black pepper

Chopped dill, flat-leaf parsley, basil, and/or chives, for garnish

When I was about five years old, my nana gave me a bunny costume to wear during my Easter egg hunt. Little did she know that it would become my outfit of choice for the following month. I wore that number to play dates. I wore it to church. I wore it to school. Heck, I even wore it to our local fruit and veg mart, where a kindly grocer gave me free carrots to snack on while my mom and I shopped. To this day, those gifted carrots are the sweetest I've ever tasted, but these roasted roots with a dressing made of all things green give even them a run for their money.

Preheat your oven to 375°F.

To roast the carrots, place them on a baking sheet. Drizzle with the oil and vinegar, season with salt and pepper, and toss well to evenly coat. Roast until tender and caramelized, 25 to 30 minutes, tossing well about halfway through.

Meanwhile, make the green sauce by placing the watercress, basil, parsley, chives, dill, and garlic in a food processor fitted with a steel blade. Pulse eight to ten times to mix and chop. Scrape down the sides of the bowl and add the lemon zest and juice, yogurt, 2 tablespoons of the goat cheese, and the Dijon and pulse until everything is finely chopped and well combined. Scrape down the sides of the bowl, pulse once more, and season with salt and pepper.

When the carrots are done, spread the green sauce mixture onto a serving plate and top with the carrots. Sprinkle on the remaining 2 tablespoons of goat cheese and a scattering of herbs.

Note:
If you don't have field carrots, regular bagged carrots will also work. Just be sure to cut larger ones lengthwise in halves or quarters for even cooking.

Sour Cream and Onion New Potato Salad

SNACKS, SIDES, SWEETS, AND SIPS · SERVES 4 TO 6

25 oz new or baby yellow flesh potatoes

Kosher salt

¼ cup mayonnaise

½–¾ cup sour cream

½ teaspoon celery salt

½ teaspoon garlic powder

1 teaspoon grainy Dijon mustard

2 teaspoons apple cider vinegar

½ lemon, zested and juiced

3 green onions, thinly sliced

3 tablespoons finely chopped chives, plus more for serving

1 tablespoon finely minced shallot

2 teaspoons finely chopped capers

Black pepper

1 large handful sour cream and onion Ruffles potato chips

Food and memory are so closely linked in my life. If I want to feel like a kid again, I make my mom's mac and cheese. If I want to feel close to my nana, I make her lemon meringue pie. And if I want to feel like I'm dancing in the basement with my dad to The Stranglers, I open up a bag of sour cream and onion Ruffles.

This one goes out to the one, the only, Ken Berg.

Place the potatoes in a large saucepan, halving any larger ones so they're all about the size of a golf ball, and cover with cool tap water by about 1 inch. Season the water well with salt and bring to a boil, uncovered, over medium-high heat. Cook just until tender, about 10 to 15 minutes, then drain and set aside to cool to room temperature.

In a large bowl, whisk together the mayonnaise, ½ cup of sour cream, celery salt, garlic powder, Dijon, vinegar, and lemon zest and juice. Stir in the green onions, chives, shallots, and capers and season well with pepper.

When the potatoes are cool, add them to the sour cream and onion mixture and toss well to combine, adding up to another ¼ cup of sour cream if needed. Season with more salt and pepper, if desired, and transfer the potato salad to a serving dish. Using your hands, roughly crush and crumble the Ruffles over the potato salad and scatter with a few chopped chives.

Strawberry Rhubarb Tarte Tatin

SNACKS, SIDES, SWEETS, AND SIPS · SERVES 8

1 quart strawberries, trimmed

2 stalks rhubarb, trimmed and cut into 1-inch pieces

1 tablespoon cornstarch

2 sheets frozen puff pastry, thawed

½ cup sugar

¼ cup butter

2 teaspoons vanilla extract or pulp of 1 vanilla bean, divided

1 cup whipping (35%) cream

½ cup sour cream

3 tablespoons icing sugar

Note:

As the strawberries and rhubarb cook down, they get quite juicy, so that's why I suggest turning this tarte out onto a rimmed serving dish.

Even though it sounds and looks pretty darn fancy, a tarte tatin is one of the quickest ways to make a stunning pie for your table. Traditionally made with apples, this springy version is a great way to put a spin on the classic combo of sweet strawberries and sour rhubarb.

Preheat your oven to 400°F, lightly grease a 9-inch round, 3-inch-deep cake pan or springform pan with cooking spray, and line the bottom with parchment paper. If using a springform pan, wrap the outside with aluminum foil to prevent leaks.

In a bowl, toss together the strawberries, rhubarb, and cornstarch until well combined, then transfer to the prepared pan. Place the pan on a baking sheet and set aside.

On a lightly floured work surface, stack the pastry sheets on top of each other and roll them lightly with a rolling pin so they adhere to each other. Cut out a 12-inch circle from the pastry, poke it about 15 to 20 times with a fork, and refrigerate it while you prepare the caramel.

In a small saucepan, combine the sugar and 1 tablespoon of water and place over medium heat. Without stirring or touching the sugar, allow the mixture to melt together and caramelize. This should take about 6 to 8 minutes. When the sugar starts to turn golden, gently swirl the pan to ensure the mixture caramelizes evenly.

As soon as the mixture is golden, turn off the heat and carefully add the butter, swirling to combine. Stir in half of the vanilla, then carefully pour the caramel over the fruit. Retrieve the puff pastry from the fridge and lay it on top of the fruit. Using a spatula, tuck the overhanging pastry down between the edge of the pan and the fruit.

Bake the tarte until the pastry is puffed and golden brown, 30 to 35 minutes. Allow the tarte to cool in the pan for 5 minutes, then carefully invert it onto a rimmed serving dish to cool completely.

Meanwhile, in a mixing bowl, or a stand mixer fitted with a whisk attachment, whip together the whipping cream, sour cream, icing sugar, and remaining vanilla just until stiff, about 2 to 3 minutes.

Serve the sliced tarte topped with the whipped cream. This is best fresh, but leftovers can be stored, covered, in the fridge for up to 2 days.

Meyer Lemon Panna Cotta

SNACKS, SIDES, SWEETS, AND SIPS · SERVES 4

¾ cup whipping (35%) cream

½ cup milk

¼ cup sugar

2 Meyer lemons (or 1 regular lemon), zested

¼ vanilla bean, scraped, or ½ teaspoon vanilla extract

1½ teaspoons unflavored gelatin powder

¼ cup sour cream

Fresh strawberries, for serving

My sister-in-law, Jenna, is my official taste tester. Sitting at our dinner table at least twice a week, she has the ability to articulate the little things that can take a dish from good to great. Essentially, she is a flavor wizard and I don't know where I'd be without her. She described this panna cotta as "soft lemons," and I don't think I can come up with a better phrase than that.

In a small saucepan set over medium heat, whisk together the cream, milk, sugar, and lemon zest as well as the vanilla bean pulp and pod (if using) and bring to a simmer. Whisk frequently and cook just until the sugar has dissolved, about 3 minutes. Discard the vanilla pod and turn the heat down to low.

Meanwhile, in a small bowl containing 1½ tablespoons of cold water, sprinkle in the gelatin powder and allow it to sit for 3 minutes to soften and bloom. After 3 minutes, the mixture should be well gelled and you shouldn't see any powdery granules on the top. If you do, use your fingertips to drip a few more drops of water onto the mixture and set aside for another 1 to 2 minutes. Add the bloomed gelatin to the cream mixture and whisk well to combine. If you're using vanilla extract, stir it in now. Remove the pot from the heat and allow to cool for about 5 minutes.

Whisk in the sour cream and pour the panna cotta mixture through a fine mesh sieve to remove any lumps, then divide into four glasses or ramekins. Transfer the panna cottas to the fridge and chill, uncovered, until set, at least 5 hours but preferably overnight. Once set, these will last tightly covered in the fridge for up to 3 days, making them a perfect get-ahead treat.

Serve topped with fresh strawberries.

Poppy Seed Cake

SNACKS, SIDES, SWEETS, AND SIPS · MAKES 1 TUBE CAKE

FOR THE CAKE

2 cups sugar

2 eggs

1 cup vegetable oil

2 cups all-purpose flour

1 cup poppy seeds

1 tablespoon baking powder

1 teaspoon kosher salt

1¼ cups evaporated milk

1 teaspoon vanilla extract

½ teaspoon almond extract

FOR THE STREUSEL

6 tablespoons all-purpose flour

6 tablespoons sugar

2 teaspoons poppy seeds

½ teaspoon kosher salt

¼ cup butter, room temperature

¼ teaspoon vanilla extract

¼ teaspoon almond extract

This dense cake is a family classic and a bit of a chameleon in terms of when we eat it. I've had it with brunch, as an afternoon pick-me-up with tea, and set on a cake pedestal for an unassuming and delicious dessert. It weighs approximately 29 pounds, serves a crowd, and lasts for days and days at room temperature and even longer in the freezer. My only tip for eating this cake is to make sure you have lots of floss and toothpicks handy, or, at the very least, that you're enjoying it with friends who will keep an eye out for latent poppy seeds stuck in your teeth.

Preheat your oven to 350°F and grease a 10-inch tube or Bundt pan with cooking spray.

For the cake, in a mixing bowl, or a stand mixer fitted with a paddle attachment, beat the sugar, eggs, and oil on high speed until well combined and the sugar starts to break down a little, about 2 to 3 minutes.

In a separate bowl, whisk together the flour, poppy seeds, baking powder, and salt until well combined. In a glass measuring cup, combine the evaporated milk with both extracts.

Mixing on low speed, add the dry ingredients to the sugar and oil mixture in three additions, alternating with two additions of the evaporated milk. When everything is incorporated, transfer the batter to the prepared pan and set aside.

Make the streusel by stirring together the flour, sugar, poppy seeds, and salt. Add the butter and both extracts and, using your hands, rub and snap the butter in until you have a crumbly streusel.

Scatter the streusel evenly over the cake batter and bake until a skewer inserted into the cake comes out clean, 1 hour and 25 minutes to 1 hour and 35 minutes. Allow the cake to cool for 30 minutes in the pan, then, after running a knife around the outside, turn it out, flip it over, and let cool completely, streusel-side up, on a wire rack.

Store the cake at room temperature, wrapped well, for up to 1 week or in the freezer for up to 2 months.

Chocolate Orange Clafoutis

SNACKS, SIDES, SWEETS, AND SIPS · SERVES 6 TO 8

4 tablespoons butter, divided

4 eggs

½ cup sugar

½ teaspoon kosher salt

1 cup milk

1 orange, zested

1½ teaspoons vanilla extract

½ cup all-purpose flour

¼ cup Dutch process cocoa powder

1 pint strawberries, trimmed and quartered

Icing sugar, for serving

The texture of clafoutis is like the perfect balance between a crêpe, flan, and crème caramel with a bit of a nod to pound cake. It's like nothing else, and that is such a good thing.

Preheat your oven to 350°F and butter a 9-inch ceramic or glass pie plate with 1 tablespoon of the butter. Melt the remaining 3 tablespoons of butter and set aside to cool slightly.

In a large bowl, whisk together the eggs, sugar, and salt. While whisking, slowly pour in the milk, followed by the orange zest, vanilla, and melted butter. Sift the flour and cocoa powder over top and whisk well so that no lumps remain. Scatter the strawberries into the prepared pie plate, then pour the batter over top.

Gently transfer the clafoutis to the oven and bake until the edges are puffed and the middle is almost set, 35 to 40 minutes. Allow the clafoutis to cool slightly, or all the way to room temperature, dust it with icing sugar, and slice it into wedges for serving. Store any leftovers tightly covered in the fridge for up to 4 days.

Pistachio Sponge Cakes with Matcha Cream

SNACKS, SIDES, SWEETS, AND SIPS · MAKES 12 MINI CAKES

FOR THE CAKES

2 eggs, separated

½ cup sugar, divided

6 tablespoons butter, room temperature

2 tablespoons sour cream

½ teaspoon vanilla extract

⅓ cup shelled unsalted pistachios

¾ cup all-purpose flour

½ teaspoon baking powder

½ teaspoon baking soda

⅛ teaspoon kosher salt

FOR THE MATCHA CREAM

½ cup brick-style cream cheese, room temperature

3 tablespoons icing sugar

½ cup whipping (35%) cream

½ teaspoon vanilla extract

¾ teaspoon matcha powder, divided

2 tablespoons chopped unsalted pistachios

6 strawberries, halved

For as long as I can remember, I've been partial to cupcakes. What's not to love about getting a whole cake all to myself?! With this recipe, I wanted to celebrate the humble cupcake by flipping it on its head and turning it into a snazzy dessert worthy of any dinner party.

Preheat your oven to 350°F and grease a 12-cup muffin tin with cooking spray.

For the cakes, whip the egg whites in a clean metal or glass mixing bowl with a hand mixer on medium-high speed until soft peaks form, about 1 minute. With the mixer running, sprinkle in 2 tablespoons of the sugar and continue to whip until stiff, about 1 to 2 more minutes.

In a separate bowl, beat the butter and remaining sugar on high speed until well combined and a little fluffy, about 2 minutes. Scrape down the bowl and add the egg yolks one at a time, scraping the bowl and beating well between each addition. Beat in the sour cream and vanilla and set aside.

Place the pistachios in a food processor fitted with a steel blade and pulse until finely ground, about 10 to 12 times. Add the flour, baking powder, baking soda, and salt and pulse once or twice just to combine.

Very gently fold one-third of the egg whites into the butter mixture, just until almost combined, followed by half of the pistachio mixture. Fold in half of the remaining whites, the remaining pistachio mixture, and then the remaining whites.

Divide the batter into your prepared muffin tin and bake until a skewer inserted into the center of a cake comes out clean, 15 to 18 minutes. Allow the cakes to cool completely in the pan before running a knife around the outsides to loosen them. Turn them out onto a work surface or serving plate.

Now make the matcha cream. In a large bowl, whip the cream cheese and icing sugar on high speed until smooth, about 1 minute. Add the whipping cream, vanilla, and ¼ teaspoon of the matcha powder and whip until medium peaks form, about 1 to 2 minutes. Using a large tablespoon or piping bag, pipe or dollop some matcha cream on each upturned cake, then, using a small sieve or a tea ball, dust the tops with the remaining matcha powder. Sprinkle each cake with chopped pistachios and top with half a strawberry. These cakes will keep tightly covered in the fridge for up to 3 days. Take them out of the fridge 30 minutes before enjoying to allow the cakes to soften slightly.

Almond Orange Cake with Roasted Rhubarb

SNACKS, SIDES, SWEETS, AND SIPS · MAKES 1 (8-INCH) TEA CAKE

FOR THE CAKE

2 tablespoons + 2 cups almond flour, divided

4 eggs, separated

½ cup sugar, divided

½ orange, zested

¼ teaspoon almond extract

¼ cup butter, melted

¼ teaspoon kosher salt

FOR THE RHUBARB

4 cups rhubarb, sliced on a diagonal into 1-inch pieces

¼ cup sugar

½ orange, zested and juiced

FOR THE TOPPING

½ cup whipping (35%) cream

2 tablespoons sour cream

¼ teaspoon vanilla extract

1–2 tablespoons icing sugar

¼ cup sliced almonds, toasted

Note:

As with some other gluten-free baking, this cake may appear to be a little dense and verging on overcooked when you pull it from the oven, but looks can be deceiving. It is light and fluffy, with an excellent toothy crumb.

During spring, the tail end of citrus season butts up against the beginning of rhubarb season, making this single-layer tea cake perfect for a weeknight bake or the final bites of a casual "Orange You Glad Winter Is Over?!" dinner party. Gluten-free and Passover-friendly, this is one of my go-tos for an understated, easy spring dessert.

Preheat your oven to 350°F and lightly grease an 8-inch round cake or springform pan with cooking spray. Line the bottom of the pan with a round of parchment paper and scatter 2 tablespoons of almond flour into the pan. Tap the flour around the sides of the pan so that it sticks to the greased sides and set aside.

For the cake, in a mixing bowl, or a stand mixer fitted with a whisk attachment, whip the egg whites on high speed until soft peaks form, about 1 minute. While continuing to whip, gradually sprinkle in ¼ cup of the sugar and whip until stiff peaks form, about 1 to 2 more minutes. Set the egg whites aside.

Whip the egg yolks with the remaining ¼ cup of sugar until pale, light, and fluffy, about 1 to 2 minutes. Whip in the orange zest and almond extract, then, with the mixer running, slowly stream in the melted butter. Whip for another minute just to combine. Fold the remaining 2 cups of almond flour and the salt into the yolk mixture, followed by one-third of the egg whites. Gently fold in half of the remaining whites, followed by the final addition, being careful not to lose too much volume.

Carefully transfer the batter to the prepared pan and bake until the cake is set in the middle and golden brown, and a skewer inserted into the center comes out clean, 25 to 30 minutes. Allow to cool completely in the pan.

While the cake bakes, prepare the rhubarb by stirring together the rhubarb, sugar, and orange zest. Allow it to sit at room temperature for 20 to 25 minutes so the rhubarb can release some of its juices. Transfer the rhubarb and all of its juices to a baking sheet and roast until tender and juicy, 20 to 25 minutes, tossing once about halfway through.

For the topping, whip together the whipping cream, sour cream, vanilla, and icing sugar on high speed just until stiff. Slice and serve the cake topped with a dollop of the cream, a spoonful of roasted rhubarb, and some sliced almonds. Tightly wrap any leftover cake and store at room temperature for up to 4 days.

Hazelnut Espresso Torte

SNACKS, SIDES, SWEETS, AND SIPS · MAKES 1 TUBE CAKE

FOR THE CAKE

⅔ cup whole hazelnuts

5 eggs, separated

1 cup sugar, divided

2 teaspoons instant espresso powder

1 tablespoon hazelnut liqueur

1 teaspoon vanilla extract

¾ cup all-purpose flour

1 teaspoon baking powder

½ teaspoon kosher salt

FOR THE CREAM

2 cups whipping (35%) cream, divided

¼ cup chocolate hazelnut spread

3 tablespoons icing sugar

2 teaspoons instant espresso powder

2 teaspoons hazelnut liqueur

¼ cup chocolate-covered espresso beans, roughly chopped

Note:

The ground hazelnuts in this batter will cause the center of the cake to fall quite a bit, even with the inverted cooling position, but that's okay! It will all be fixed once you layer and fill the cake.

There is a legendary family story that goes with this torte involving a family party, lots of Prosecco, a very hormonal teenaged Mary, and my cousin Molly taking creative license in secretly redecorating my masterpiece. Her brazen act of dessert vandalism led to me flinging myself on a bed in one of the Top 10 angst-induced fits of my youth. Luckily, I have since found the humor in this classic Foote family prank, as this story seems to come up at every big hoopla we've had since.

Preheat your oven to 325°F and lightly grease a 10-inch removable-bottom tube pan with cooking spray. Scatter a few tablespoons of flour into the pan and tap it around to coat, dumping out any excess flour.

For the cake, in a large skillet set over medium heat, toast the hazelnuts until they smell nutty and just start to brown. This won't take long. Transfer the hazelnuts to a food processor fitted with a steel blade and set aside to cool completely.

In a mixing bowl, or a stand mixer fitted with a whisk attachment, whip the egg whites on high speed until soft peaks form, about 1 minute. With the mixer running, slowly sprinkle in ½ cup of the sugar and continue to whip the whites until stiff, about 2 to 3 minutes. Transfer the whites to a clean bowl and add the yolks to the same bowl you whipped the whites in (no need to wipe it out). With the mixer running on low speed, sprinkle in the remaining ½ cup sugar and mix to combine. Turn the speed up to high and whip until the egg yolks have tripled in volume and are light and pale yellow. In a small bowl, dissolve the espresso powder in the hazelnut liqueur and vanilla, then whip the mixture into the egg yolks and set aside.

Blitz the hazelnuts in the food processor until finely ground, then add the flour, baking powder, and salt and pulse a few times to combine. Add half of this mixture to the whipped yolks and gently fold together. Fold in half of the egg whites until almost combined, followed by the remaining hazelnut mixture. Very gently fold in the remaining whites just until combined. Transfer the mixture to the prepared tube pan and bake until a skewer inserted into the center of the cake comes out clean, 50 to 55 minutes.

Invert the pan over a wire rack or on a wine bottle and allow it to cool completely. When cool, run a sharp knife around the outside of the cake and the center tube of the pan. Remove the cake and inner portion of the pan, then run the knife under the bottom of the cake to fully release it. Once out of the pan, use a large serrated knife to cut the cake horizontally into two to three layers and set aside.

For the cream, place 1 cup of the cream and the chocolate hazelnut spread in a mixing bowl, or a stand mixer fitted with a whisk attachment, and whip on high speed until stiff peaks form. Remove from the bowl and set aside. Whip the remaining 1 cup of cream with the icing sugar on high speed until stiff peaks form. In a small bowl, combine the espresso powder with the hazelnut liqueur, add it to the sweetened whipped cream mixture, and whip in.

Gently swirl the two whipped creams together and assemble the cake by sandwiching the layers together with the cream mixture. Top the cake with the cream mixture and scatter on the chopped espresso beans. Serve immediately or cover and keep in the fridge for up to 4 days.

Sailor's Warning

SNACKS, SIDES, SWEETS, AND SIPS · MAKES 1 COCKTAIL

3½ oz Lambrusco, chilled

2 oz blood orange juice

A twist of blood orange zest or a slice of blood orange, for garnish

Note:

This is a great recipe to do in a large batch. Just combine a 750 ml bottle of chilled Lambrusco with the juice of 7 or 8 blood oranges in a large pitcher, stir well to combine, and refrigerate until ready to serve.

A crafty way to sneak a bit of bubbly into your morning meal, I've given the classic Mimosa a bit of a spin with the addition of blood orange juice and ruby red Lambrusco. As with any mid- to late-morning drink, an old-timey warning should come in tow. So, as the saying goes:

Red sky at night, sailors' delight

Red sky at morning, sailors' warning

In a champagne flute, combine the Lambrusco and blood orange juice, being careful not to let it bubble over. Garnish with a twist of blood orange zest or a slice of blood orange and enjoy immediately.

Ginger Pimm's

SNACKS, SIDES, SWEETS, AND SIPS · MAKES 1 COCKTAIL

Ice cubes

2 oz Pimm's

1 oz orange juice

½ oz lime juice

½ oz lemon juice

¾ cup ginger ale

Citrus peel or rounds, for garnish

Inspired by my friends Renée and Kyle, and their love of a Pimm's cup, this gingery cocktail takes advantage of the last days of citrus season.

Half-fill a highball glass with ice cubes. Pour over the Pimm's and all the juices, and stir well to chill and combine. Top with the ginger ale and garnish with a few citrus peels or rounds.

Tarragon Greyhound

Ice cubes

½ oz tarragon simple syrup
  (see below)

2 oz vodka

4 oz grapefruit juice

2 lime wedges

Tarragon sprig, for garnish

The colors and flavors of this bright, slightly licorice-y cocktail are the perfect way to toast the warming days and new growth of spring.

Half-fill a highball glass with ice cubes and pour over the tarragon simple syrup, vodka, and grapefruit juice. Squeeze in the juice of 1 lime wedge and stir well to combine.

Garnish with the remaining lime wedge and a sprig of fresh tarragon.

Tarragon Simple Syrup

MAKES ABOUT ¾ CUP

½ cup sugar

3 sprigs tarragon

In a small saucepan, combine the sugar and tarragon with ½ cup of water. Bring the mixture to a simmer over medium heat and cook, stirring occasionally, until the sugar is dissolved, about 3 to 5 minutes.

Cool the simple syrup to room temperature, discard the tarragon sprigs, and transfer to a container. Seal the container and refrigerate for up to 1 month.

Summer

Bright, Fresh, and Classic

Cottage Pancakes

BREAKFAST THROUGH DINNER · MAKES 12 TO 15 PANCAKES

2 cups all-purpose flour

3 tablespoons sugar

1½ teaspoons baking powder

¾ teaspoon baking soda

½ teaspoon kosher salt

¼ teaspoon freshly grated nutmeg

3 tablespoons butter, plus more for cooking and serving

1¾ cups buttermilk

1 teaspoon vanilla extract

3 eggs, separated

1 tablespoon canola oil

1 cup fresh (not frozen) blueberries

Maple syrup, for serving

In my last cookbook, *Kitchen Party*, I included a recipe for my favorite for-a-crowd pancakes. Those lemon poppy seed Dutch babies continue to be on regular rotation when all of our cottage beds are filled, but when it's just my mom, Aaron, and me, these are the pancakes that make their way onto our breakfast bar.

Set a large nonstick skillet over medium-low heat, place a baking sheet in your oven, and preheat the oven to 200°F.

In a large bowl, sift together the flour, sugar, baking powder, baking soda, salt, and nutmeg and whisk well to combine. Melt the butter in the warm skillet. Add the melted butter to the flour mixture, along with the buttermilk, vanilla, and egg yolks. Stir just until barely combined and lots of lumps remain.

In a separate bowl, whisk the egg whites until medium peaks form, about 1 to 2 minutes, then fold them into the batter in two additions, just until combined but some lumps remain.

Add a pat of butter and a little oil to the preheated pan and spoon in about ¼ cup of batter per pancake. Scatter the top of each pancake with some blueberries and cook until bubbles appear on top and the underside is golden brown, 1 to 2 minutes. Flip the pancakes and continue to cook until both sides are golden brown, about another 1 to 2 minutes, then transfer to the baking sheet in the oven. Continue cooking the pancakes, adding more butter and oil to the pan before each batch, until all of the batter has been used.

Serve with even more butter and a healthy drizzle of pure maple syrup.

Note:
Separate any leftover pancakes with a small square of parchment paper, place in a resealable freezer bag, and freeze for up to 1 month. To reheat, simply pop them in the toaster.

A Classic Lobster Roll (with Chips because Duh)

BREAKFAST THROUGH DINNER · SERVES 4

5 (each 6 oz) lobster tails

3 tablespoons butter, divided

½ teaspoon seafood seasoning, such as Old Bay

⅓ cup mayonnaise

½ lemon, zested and juiced

¼ cup finely minced celery

2 tablespoons finely chopped flat-leaf parsley

2 tablespoons finely chopped chives, plus more for serving

2 tablespoons finely chopped tarragon

Kosher salt and black pepper

4 split-top buns

Wavy-cut potato chips, such as Ruffles

Celery leaves (optional)

Lobster rolls are perhaps the most decadent and quintessential sandwiches of summer. In my version, sweet hunks of fresh lobster are tossed in a flavorful mayonnaise dressing with a ton of fresh herbs and the added crunch of some wavy-cut potato chips—a trick developed by a young Mary Berg to improve most bun-based sandwiches.

First, remove the meat from the lobster tails. Cut down the tops of the shells with kitchen shears, remove the vein with a damp piece of paper towel, and, holding a tail wrapped in a clean kitchen towel, squeeze it to crack open the shell. Remove the meat, dice it into large bite-sized pieces, and set aside. Repeat with the remaining lobster tails.

Warm a skillet over medium heat and add 1 tablespoon of the butter to melt. When melted, add the diced lobster meat and seafood seasoning and cook just until the lobster is opaque, about 3 to 4 minutes. Remove the lobster from the pan and refrigerate to cool completely.

In a mixing bowl, stir together the mayonnaise, lemon zest and juice, celery, parsley, chives, and tarragon. Fold in the chilled lobster meat and season with salt and pepper. Set the lobster back in the fridge while you toast the buns.

Place a large skillet over medium heat and spread the outsides of the buns with the remaining 2 tablespoons of butter. Toast the buns in the hot pan until golden brown on both sides, about 2 minutes per side.

To serve, fill the rolls with the lobster, crush some chips over top, and sprinkle on some finely chopped chives and celery leaves (if using).

Grilled Summer Squash Pizza

BREAKFAST THROUGH DINNER · SERVES 6 TO 8

FOR THE PESTO

2 cups loosely packed basil

¼ cup loosely packed flat-leaf parsley

1 garlic clove, finely minced

¼ cup finely grated Parmigiano-Reggiano cheese

1½ tablespoons pine nuts

½ lemon, zested and juiced

3 tablespoons olive oil

Kosher salt and black pepper

FOR THE CHEESE

1 cup ricotta cheese

¼ cup finely grated Parmigiano-Reggiano cheese

2 garlic cloves, finely minced

½ lemon, zested and juiced

Kosher salt and black pepper

FOR THE PIZZA

½ green zucchini, thinly sliced

½ yellow zucchini or squash, thinly sliced

3 tablespoons olive oil, divided

Kosher salt and black pepper

6–8 squash blossoms

½ cup pitted green olives (optional)

8 thin slices smoked prosciutto (optional)

1 ball store-bought pizza dough or My Favorite Delivery pizza dough (page 146)

Crushed red pepper flakes, for serving

Anyone who grows a vegetable garden or peruses the stalls of farmers' markets during the summer months knows that zucchini and summer squash are prolific growers. This grilled pizza is a great way to use up a bumper crop of these thin-skinned cultivars. Feel free to swap out the zucchini or yellow squash with other long summer squashes such as cousas or zephyrs, or even a handful or two of tender pattypans. On a related note: How am I just now realizing that most summer squashes sound like they could be Frank Zappa's children?

Preheat your grill to medium heat.

Prepare the pesto by placing the basil, parsley, garlic, Parmigiano-Reggiano, pine nuts, lemon zest and juice, and oil in a food processor fitted with a steel blade and blending until smooth. Season with salt and pepper and set aside.

For the cheese, stir the ricotta, Parmigiano-Reggiano, garlic, and lemon zest and juice together in a small bowl. Season with salt and pepper and set aside.

Prepare the pizza toppings by tossing both zucchini together with 1 tablespoon of the oil. Season with salt and pepper. Using your fingers, pinch out and discard the stamens from the inside of the squash blossoms and set the blossoms aside. Roughly chop the olives and tear the prosciutto into large bite-sized pieces (if using).

Lightly flour a work surface and roll or stretch the pizza dough into a large circle, about 16 inches in diameter. Brush the surface of the dough with 1 tablespoon of the remaining oil and gently lift and drape the dough onto the preheated grill, oil-side down. Close the lid and cook for 2 minutes. Check the underside of the crust. If it's not golden brown, leave it for another 1 to 2 minutes.

When the bottom of the crust is golden and grilled, brush the top of the dough with a little more oil and, using a pair of tongs, carefully flip the crust. Top the grilled side of the pizza with the pesto and prepared zucchini and dot the ricotta mixture over top. Scatter over the squash blossoms and the olives and prosciutto (if using). Turn the heat down to medium-low, close the lid of the grill, and cook until the bottom of the crust is golden and grilled and the toppings have softened slightly, 2 to 3 minutes.

Transfer the pizza to a large wooden cutting board, season with salt and red pepper flakes, and cut into 10 to 12 slices.

Sesame Soba with Peanut Sauce

BREAKFAST THROUGH DINNER · SERVES 4

FOR THE NOODLES

8 oz soba noodles

2 limes

2 teaspoons soy sauce

1 tablespoon toasted sesame oil

2 tablespoons sesame seeds, toasted

½ English cucumber

1 large carrot

1 bell pepper

4 green onions

1 lb firm tofu

¼ cup chopped roasted peanuts, for garnish

¼ cup picked cilantro leaves, for garnish

FOR THE PEANUT SAUCE

¾ cup natural peanut butter

¼ cup hoisin sauce

¼ cup soy sauce

2 teaspoons fish sauce

1–2 tablespoons sriracha

2 tablespoons grated fresh ginger

1 garlic clove, finely minced

On those sweltering summer days when the mere thought of standing near a hot stove is met with a scoff, this quick veg-filled soba bowl with peanut sauce is all I crave.

For the noodles, bring a large pot of salted water to a boil over high heat and cook according to the package directions or until al dente. While they're cooking, place the juice of 1 lime along with the soy sauce, sesame oil, and toasted sesame seeds in a large bowl and whisk to combine. When the noodles are done cooking, drain and rinse them under cold water to remove the outer layer of starch. Add to the soy sauce mixture, toss well to combine, and set aside.

Prepare your vegetables and tofu by cutting the cucumber and carrot into 3-inch-long matchsticks, thinly slicing the bell pepper and green onions, and cutting the tofu into ½-inch dice. Quarter the remaining lime and then set this all aside.

For the peanut sauce, place the peanut butter, hoisin sauce, soy sauce, fish sauce, and sriracha in a mixing bowl and whisk to combine. Add the ginger and garlic along with 2 to 4 tablespoons of water to reach a thick but pourable consistency.

To serve, divide the dressed soba noodles between four shallow bowls and arrange the prepared vegetables and tofu on top. Pour on the peanut sauce and garnish with the chopped roasted peanuts, cilantro leaves, and a lime wedge. Store any leftover peanut sauce in a jar or a resealable container in the fridge for up to 2 weeks.

Grilled Tuna Panzanella Niçoise

BREAKFAST THROUGH DINNER · SERVES 4

FOR THE SALAD

4 eggs

12 oz mini potatoes

Kosher salt

2 small shallots, peeled and each cut into 6 wedges

4 tablespoons olive oil, divided

Black pepper

12 oz cherry tomatoes

8 oz green beans, trimmed

3–4 tablespoons butter

4 thick slices crusty bread

4 (each about 6 oz) sushi-grade tuna steaks

1 teaspoon herbes de Provence

4–5 large handfuls baby arugula

½ cup Niçoise or other small black olives

¼ cup capers, drained

¼ cup finely chopped flat-leaf parsley

FOR THE DRESSING

¼ cup white wine vinegar

2 tablespoons lemon juice (about 1 lemon)

1 tablespoon Dijon mustard

2 teaspoons honey

1 garlic clove, finely minced

2 anchovy fillets, finely minced

½ teaspoon herbes de Provence

¼ cup extra virgin olive oil

Kosher salt and black pepper

Any time I serve salad as a main, my brain likes to play that "You don't win friends with salad" conga line scene from *The Simpsons* on a loop. You might not win over anyone with salad as a meal if it's a bowl of mixed greens and plain vinaigrette, but both Niçoise and panzanella are definitely friendship-worthy salads. The classic Niçoise gets a savory boost in this recipe from the grill and, just to really put this salad into meal territory, I've done a mash-up with a Tuscan panzanella by adding big hunks of crusty bread.

Preheat your grill to medium and hard-boil the eggs (see page 29 for how to perfectly hard-boil eggs).

In a medium pot, cover the potatoes with 1 inch of cool tap water and season well with salt. Bring the potatoes to a boil over medium-high heat and cook until barely tender, about 8 to 10 minutes. Drain and transfer the potatoes to a mixing bowl. Add the shallots and drizzle with 2 tablespoons of the oil. Season with salt and pepper and toss gently to coat.

Place a vegetable grill pan or a few layers of heavy-duty aluminum foil onto your grill and spread the potatoes and shallots into an even layer. Close the lid and cook for 20 minutes, stirring every few minutes or so.

Meanwhile, toss the tomatoes and green beans with 1 tablespoon of the oil and season with salt and pepper. After 20 minutes, add the tomatoes and beans to the potatoes and shallots, close the lid, and continue to cook until the beans are tender and the tomatoes are a little charred, another 5 to 10 minutes.

Evenly spread the butter over both sides of each slice of bread and place them on the grill to toast and char, about 2 to 3 minutes per side. Remove the bread, cut into roughly 1-inch cubes, and set aside.

For the tuna, turn the heat on your grill up to medium-high and drizzle both sides of the tuna steaks with the remaining 1 tablespoon of oil. Season with salt and pepper and evenly scatter on the herbes de Provence. Grill the tuna for 2 minutes per side for rare, or longer if you prefer medium. Allow the tuna to rest for about 1 to 2 minutes, then slice against the grain into ½-inch-thick slices.

Prepare the dressing by whisking the vinegar, lemon juice, Dijon, and honey with the garlic, anchovies, and herbes de Provence. Slowly whisk in the oil and season with salt and pepper.

Transfer the grilled vegetables and bread cubes to a large bowl, toss with half of the dressing, and set aside for 2 to 3 minutes to allow the flavors to meld.

To assemble the salad, divide the arugula between four plates, or place on a serving dish, and top with the grilled vegetables and bread cubes. Peel and halve the hardboiled eggs and add them along with the olives, capers, grilled tuna, and a scattering of parsley to the salad, and drizzle with the remaining dressing.

Chicken Parmesan Saltimbocca with Sautéed Tomatoes and Fresh Mozzarella

BREAKFAST THROUGH DINNER · SERVES 4

FOR THE CHICKEN

4 boneless, skinless chicken breasts

Kosher salt and black pepper

12–16 thin slices prosciutto

8–12 large basil leaves

2 garlic cloves, very finely minced

¼ cup all-purpose flour

2 eggs

1 cup panko breadcrumbs

½ cup ground Parmigiano-Reggiano cheese (see note)

2 tablespoons butter

2 tablespoons olive oil

FOR THE TOMATOES AND MOZZARELLA

1 tablespoon olive oil

12 oz cherry tomatoes, halved

Kosher salt and black pepper

1 garlic clove, finely minced

1 teaspoon balsamic vinegar

6–7 oz fresh mozzarella, roughly torn

¼ cup finely chopped basil

Chicken Parmesan, or, as we call it in our house, Chick Parm, has always been one of Aaron's absolute favorites. While it's typically a dish I make in the colder months of the year, I wanted to freshen up the classic by using sautéed summer tomatoes in place of the usual slow-cooked sauce and put a new spin on the chicken with a nod to the Italian dish saltimbocca. That is to say, wrapping it in fresh herbs and prosciutto before breading and frying. I mean, what could be bad about that?

Preheat your oven to 200°F and place a large baking sheet lined with a wire rack on the middle rack.

Prepare the chicken breasts by lightly pounding them with a meat mallet until even in thickness. You want them about ½-inch thick. Season both sides of the chicken with salt and pepper and set aside.

Lay 3 to 4 slices of prosciutto on a work surface so that they overlap and are big enough to wrap around a chicken breast. Place 2 or 3 basil leaves on the prosciutto and scatter over one-quarter of the garlic. Lay on a chicken breast and wrap the prosciutto around it. Set aside and continue with the remaining prosciutto, basil, garlic, and chicken.

Place a large skillet over medium-high heat. While it heats, place the flour in a shallow dish and season with salt and pepper. In a separate shallow dish, beat the eggs until well combined. In a third shallow dish, combine the panko and ground Parmigiano-Reggiano.

Place 1 tablespoon each of the butter and oil in the skillet, turning the heat down to medium if the fat starts to smoke. Dredge 2 pieces of chicken in the flour mixture, making sure to tap off any excess, then dip into the egg, and, finally, press into the breadcrumb mixture. Carefully add the chicken to the hot pan and cook, undisturbed, on the first side until golden brown and the coating is set, 3 to 4 minutes. Flip the chicken over and cook until cooked through and golden brown all over, another 2 to 3 minutes. Remove the chicken to the rack-lined baking sheet in the oven to keep warm.

Note:

To avoid burning, use ground Parmigiano-Reggiano rather than grated for this recipe. Ground Parmigiano-Reggiano can be found in the deli and cheese section of most grocery stores, or you can make it yourself by pulsing a chunk of Parm in a food processor until finely ground.

Add the remaining 1 tablespoon each of the butter and oil to the pan and coat and cook the final 2 pieces of chicken. Transfer them to the oven to keep warm as well.

For the tomatoes, turn the heat down to medium and, using paper towel, wipe out any remaining oil and butter as well as any bits of burnt crust. Add the oil to the pan along with the tomatoes. Season with salt and pepper and cook, stirring frequently, until the tomatoes get a little saucy, about 3 to 4 minutes. Add the garlic and vinegar and cook just until reduced.

Serve the chicken topped with the sautéed tomatoes, mozzarella, and finely chopped basil.

Grilled Pork Tenderloin with Cherry Balsamic Chutney

BREAKFAST THROUGH DINNER · SERVES 4 TO 6

FOR THE TENDERLOINS

3 tablespoons balsamic vinegar

3 tablespoons olive oil

3 tablespoons grainy Dijon mustard

3 garlic cloves, roughly chopped

1 tablespoon kosher salt

1 teaspoon black pepper

2 sprigs rosemary

2 (each 16 oz) pork tenderloins

FOR THE CHUTNEY

1 tablespoon olive oil

1 small shallot, finely diced

Kosher salt and black pepper

1 garlic clove, finely minced

1½ teaspoons grated fresh ginger

2 cups pitted cherries, fresh or frozen and thawed

¼ cup balsamic vinegar

1½ tablespoons grainy Dijon mustard

1 tablespoon pure maple syrup

1 sprig rosemary

While there are a few diehards in my neck of the woods who fire up their grill as soon as the temperature gets above freezing, in my books, summer is the official season of grilling. Cooking outside is the perfect way to enjoy the weather and has the added benefit of not heating up your house on sweltering days. This quick marinated pork tenderloin is fast enough for a weeknight meal and, with the cherry balsamic chutney, fancy enough for an outdoor feast.

In a non-reactive bowl or baking dish large enough to hold both pork tenderloins, whisk together the balsamic, oil, Dijon, garlic, salt, and pepper. Add the rosemary and then the pork tenderloins and toss until well coated. Cover the bowl with plastic wrap and either leave the pork to marinate and come up to room temperature, about 30 minutes, or refrigerate the pork for up to 1½ hours. Just be sure to let it sit at room temperature for 30 minutes before cooking.

Meanwhile, make the chutney. Heat the oil in a small saucepan over medium heat. Add the shallots, season with salt and pepper, and cook until softened and just starting to turn golden brown, 2 minutes. Add the garlic and ginger and cook for another 30 seconds. Stir in the cherries, balsamic, Dijon, maple syrup, and then the rosemary. Turn the heat down to medium-low and simmer, uncovered, until the cherries have broken down and the chutney has thickened, 15 to 20 minutes. Discard the rosemary and keep the chutney warm over low heat or set it aside to cool to room temperature for serving.

When you're ready to cook, preheat your grill to medium. Brush the grill with oil or spritz it in short bursts with cooking spray, being sure to hold the can a safe distance from the heat. Remove the tenderloins from the marinade, shaking off any excess, and place them on the grill. Close the lid and cook until the internal temperature reaches 135°F, about 15 minutes, turning the tenderloins every 3 to 4 minutes to ensure even cooking. Remove the tenderloins from the heat, loosely cover with foil, and allow to rest for 10 minutes before slicing and serving with the cherry balsamic chutney.

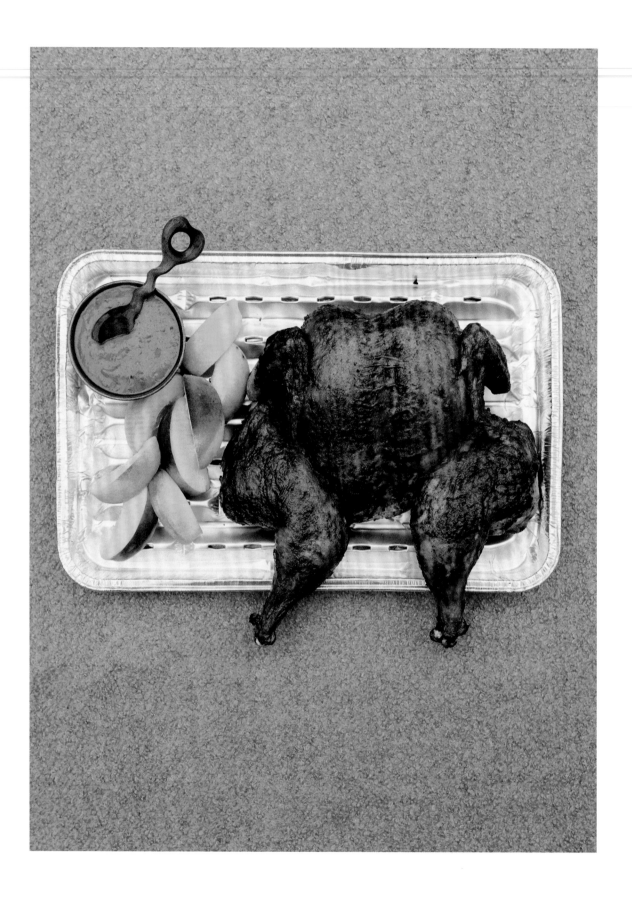

Chipotle Peach Grilled Chicken

BREAKFAST THROUGH DINNER · SERVES 4

3 tablespoons olive oil, divided

½ small yellow onion, finely diced

Kosher salt and black pepper

2 garlic cloves, roughly chopped

¼ cup light-flavored beer, such as pilsner or lager

3 ripe peaches, peeled and roughly chopped

1 (6½ oz) can of chipotles in adobo

3 tablespoons Dijon mustard

3–4 tablespoons apple cider vinegar

1 (about 3½ lb) whole chicken

½ teaspoon ground cumin

½ teaspoon smoked paprika

½ teaspoon chili powder

½ teaspoon garlic powder

For those who think that I don't make mistakes in the kitchen, this recipe proves otherwise. I used to put habaneros in this until, after one ill-fated dinner at the cottage, I touched my ear with what I thought were well-washed hands. Spoiler alert: they weren't. It hurt. A lot. To avoid making this mistake again, I swapped out the habanero for chipotle—and the recipe has never been better.

In a small saucepan, warm 1 tablespoon of the oil over medium heat. Add the onions, season with salt and pepper, and cook just until the onions are tender and translucent, 2 to 3 minutes. Add the garlic and cook for another 30 seconds to soften, then deglaze the pan with the beer. Add the peaches, 1 whole chipotle pepper, ¼ cup of the adobo sauce (storing the remaining peppers and sauce in the fridge or freezer for a later use), Dijon, and 3 tablespoons of vinegar and bring the mixture to a simmer. Turn the heat down to low and simmer, uncovered and stirring occasionally, until the peaches are well broken down and the mixture is saucy, 30 to 35 minutes. Using an immersion or stand blender, blend the peach mixture until smooth, add more salt, pepper, and vinegar to taste, and set aside.

Preheat your grill to medium.

Spatchcock the chicken by removing the backbone. To do this, flip the chicken over so that it sits breast-side down and, using a pair of kitchen shears, carefully cut along either side of the backbone. Flip the bird over and press down to flatten it. In a small bowl, mix together the cumin, paprika, chili powder, and garlic powder.

Drizzle the remaining 2 tablespoons of oil over both sides of the chicken, sprinkle on the spice mix, and season well with salt and pepper. Place the chicken on the grill bone-side down, close the lid, and cook for 30 minutes. At this point, divide the chipotle peach sauce into two bowls. Set one aside for serving. Use the other for basting the skin of the chicken every 5 minutes or so, continuing to cook until the internal temperature of the thickest part of the thigh reaches 160°F to 165°F.

Remove the chicken from the heat, cover it loosely with a piece of aluminum foil, and allow it to rest for 10 minutes. Meanwhile, warm the reserved chipotle peach sauce and serve with the chicken.

Thai Curry Trout with Pineapple Slaw

BREAKFAST THROUGH DINNER · SERVES 2 TO 3

1 butterflied rainbow trout or 2 rainbow trout fillets

Olive oil

Kosher salt

¼ cup Thai curry paste, red or yellow, store-bought or homemade (see page 91)

½ cup thinly sliced fresh pineapple

¼ red bell pepper, thinly sliced

½ shallot, thinly sliced

½–1 Thai bird's eye chili, seeded and thinly sliced

¼ cup picked cilantro leaves

1 lime, zested and juiced, plus extra wedges for garnish

This recipe is inspired by a dish that Aaron and I shared at Nopi, an Ottolenghi restaurant in London, England. By filling delicate rainbow trout with curry paste and quickly roasting it in a hot oven or on the grill, you'll get an incredibly quick, deliciously light dinner perfumed with spicy flavor, perfect for warm summer nights.

Preheat your oven to 400°F or your grill to medium-high.

Place the fish on a baking sheet or, if you're using the grill, a large piece of heavy-duty aluminum foil. Drizzle the fish with oil and season with salt. With the fish skin-side down, spread the curry paste over the flesh, and close the fish over (or lay 1 piece of fish, skin-side up, on top of the other if you're using 2 fillets).

Roast the fish in the oven, or on the grill with the lid closed, until the flesh flakes easily with a fork, 10 to 15 minutes, depending on the thickness of your trout. If using the grill, carefully flip the trout halfway through cooking.

Meanwhile, make the pineapple slaw by tossing together the pineapple, bell peppers, shallots, and chili with the cilantro. Add the lime zest and juice and 2 teaspoons of oil. Season with salt.

Cut the trout into portions, removing the skin if desired, and top with the pineapple slaw. Serve with extra lime wedges for garnish.

Yellow Thai Curry Paste

½ red bell pepper, roughly chopped

1–2 Thai bird's eye chilies, stems removed and roughly chopped

2 green onions, roughly chopped

2 garlic cloves, roughly chopped

1½-inch piece fresh ginger or galangal, peeled and finely chopped

½ stalk lemongrass, outer 2 layers discarded, finely chopped

1 tablespoon chopped cilantro stems

½ teaspoon ground turmeric

½ teaspoon ground coriander

½ teaspoon ground cumin

¼ teaspoon black pepper

2 teaspoons fish sauce

1 lime, zested and juiced

1 tablespoon coconut oil

1½ teaspoons honey

Kosher salt

Blitz the bell peppers, bird's eye chilies, green onions, garlic, ginger, lemongrass, cilantro, turmeric, coriander, cumin, pepper, fish sauce, lime zest and juice, coconut oil, and honey in a food processor fitted with a steel blade until the mixture is paste-like. Season to taste with salt and refrigerate in a glass jar for up to 1 week.

Marinated Halloumi

BREAKFAST THROUGH DINNER · SERVES 2 AS A MAIN OR 4 AS A SIDE

¼ cup extra virgin olive oil

2 tablespoons red wine vinegar

1 lemon, zested and juiced

2 garlic cloves, roughly chopped

2 tablespoons finely chopped flat-leaf parsley, plus more for serving

1 tablespoon finely chopped oregano, plus more for serving

2 teaspoons kosher salt

1 teaspoon crushed red pepper flakes

½ teaspoon black pepper

8 oz halloumi cheese, sliced into 4 equal pieces

¼ cup finely chopped oil-packed sundried tomatoes

Halloumi works perfectly as a main protein for non-meat eaters. It's a firm, slightly briny cheese originally made in Cyprus that marinates beautifully and can be grilled up to satisfy anyone's smoky cravings.

In a medium bowl, prepare a marinade by combining the oil, vinegar, lemon zest and juice, garlic, parsley, oregano, salt, red pepper flakes, and pepper. Add the halloumi and stir well to evenly coat the cheese in the marinade. Cover the bowl and place it in the fridge to marinate overnight, or for up to 24 hours.

When you're ready to cook, preheat the grill to medium-high and remove the halloumi from the marinade, shaking off any excess and reserving the marinade. Grill the halloumi until nice char marks appear and the cheese has slightly softened, 2 to 3 minutes per side.

While the halloumi grills, stir the sundried tomatoes into the reserved marinade. Transfer the halloumi to serving plates, spoon over the marinade and sundried tomatoes, and scatter with some more chopped parsley and oregano.

Fire-Burnt Baba Ghanoush

SNACKS, SIDES, SWEETS, AND SIPS · MAKES ABOUT 1½ CUPS

1 large (about 1½ lb) Italian
   eggplant

1 lemon, halved

2 garlic cloves, very finely
   minced

¼ cup tahini

¼ teaspoon smoked paprika

¼ teaspoon ground cumin

2–4 tablespoons extra virgin
   olive oil

Kosher salt and black pepper

1 tablespoon finely chopped
   flat-leaf parsley

Note:

If you are one of those lucky
people who has access to a fire
pit, try roasting the eggplant
in the hot embers of a recently
flameless fire. Just place the
pierced eggplants directly
on the hot embers and roast,
turning occasionally, until
blackened and deflated, about
18 to 25 minutes, depending
on the size of your eggplants.
The smoky flavor will permeate
the flesh, so discard the super-
charred skin before blitzing.

To all those who tend to burn things like I sometimes do after a couple glasses of wine, this recipe is for you. Burnt on purpose, this eggplant dip goes with pretty much any dippable you can think of. Crudités, toasted pita, bread, crackers, and chips come to mind, and spreading it onto a burger or serving it with the Herby Falafel (page 32) would be out-of-this-world delish.

Preheat your grill to medium-low.

Pierce the eggplant a few times with a fork, place directly on the hot grill, lower the lid, and cook, turning occasionally, until the skin is blackened and the eggplant looks deflated. This can take anywhere from 30 minutes to 1 hour, depending on its size. When charred and tender, set the eggplant aside to cool to room temperature. Grill the lemon cut-side down until well charred, about 4 to 6 minutes, and set aside with the eggplant to cool to room temperature.

Slice the cooled eggplant in half lengthwise and, using a spoon, scoop out the flesh. Reserve the charred skin of half of the eggplant. Place the flesh in a fine mesh strainer and sit it over a bowl or in the sink for 10 to 15 minutes to drain some of the juices.

Transfer the eggplant flesh to a food processor fitted with a steel blade and add the juice from the charred lemon along with the garlic, tahini, paprika, and cumin. Purée until smooth. Gradually add the oil, beginning with 2 tablespoons and slowly adding more until you reach a smooth and creamy consistency. Season with salt and pepper. Taste the eggplant dip and, if you would like a smokier flavor, add some of the reserved charred skin. Personally, I like adding the skin of half of the charred eggplant for a good, smoky flavor, but start with a little and gradually add until it tastes right to you.

Transfer the eggplant mixture to a small bowl, stir in the parsley, and drizzle over a little more oil, if desired. Store any leftovers in a reseal-able container in the fridge for up to 1 week.

Spicy Dill Quickles

SNACKS, SIDES, SWEETS, AND SIPS · MAKES ABOUT 4 CUPS

1½ lb fresh crunchy vegetables

1 handful dill sprigs, stems included

4 garlic cloves, sliced

1 red finger chili or jalapeño pepper, sliced

1 teaspoon yellow mustard seeds

1 cup white vinegar

2 tablespoons sugar

2 tablespoons kosher salt

When I was growing up, our local grocery store would hand out free cookies at the bakery counter to all the little kids. However, I had no interest in these free treats and would only be satisfied if my mom took me down the pickle aisle and popped open a jar of dills before beginning the rest of her shop. At the checkout, the cashier would often seem perplexed to find an empty jar of brine to be scanned and purchased by my nonplussed mother, while I sat smiling contentedly like the little pickle monster that I am.

Cut the vegetables into whatever shape or size you'd like, making sure they'll easily fit into a clean 4-cup glass container such as a mason jar.

If I'm using pickling cucumbers or small to medium carrots, I typically cut them into spears. Regular field cucumbers or larger carrots I slice into ½-inch rounds. Round vegetables such as fennel, beets, or radishes I cut into ½-inch-thick wedges. Thinner vegetables such as asparagus, green beans, or wax beans are perfect for pickling if trimmed and left whole.

Pack the vegetables into the container along with the dill, garlic, chili, and mustard seeds. Set aside.

In a small saucepan, combine the vinegar, sugar, and salt with 1 cup of water and set it over medium-low heat. Bring the mixture to a simmer and cook, stirring occasionally, until the sugar and salt are dissolved, about 2 to 3 minutes. Remove the mixture from the heat and set aside for 5 minutes to cool slightly.

Carefully pour the hot pickling liquid over the vegetables, making sure they're all submerged. If the vegetables are not covered by the pickling liquid, add more white vinegar and water in equal parts. Seal the container and allow it to cool to room temperature before transferring to the fridge for at least 6 hours to chill and allow the flavors to meld.

The pickles will keep in your fridge for up to 1 month.

Deep-Fried Pickles

SNACKS, SIDES, SWEETS, AND SIPS · SERVES 3 TO 4

Canola oil, for deep-frying

3–4 large dill pickles, sliced into ¼-inch rounds

¾ cup all-purpose flour, divided

¼ cup cornstarch

½ teaspoon kosher salt

½ teaspoon smoked paprika

¼ teaspoon black pepper

¼ teaspoon garlic powder

4 teaspoons finely chopped dill, divided

½ cup cold light-flavored beer, such as pilsner or lager

1 cup panko breadcrumbs

¼ cup mayonnaise

¼ cup sour cream

½ lemon, zested and juiced

Cayenne pepper hot sauce, such as Tabasco

As I've mentioned, I'm a bit of a pickle monster. Sweet, sour, quick pickled, or slow fermented, I'll eat them any which way I can get them, but I can't think of a better pickle treat than deep-fried.

In a large Dutch oven or deep sauté pan, heat 1 inch of oil over medium-high heat to 365°F to 375°F. If you do not have a thermometer, heat the oil until it shimmers or the end of a wooden spoon causes bubbles to form when gently dipped into it. Place a wire rack over a baking sheet and set aside.

While the oil comes up to temperature, lay the pickle slices out on a piece of paper towel and dry them well. In a large bowl, whisk together ½ cup of the flour with the cornstarch, salt, paprika, pepper, and garlic powder. Stir in 2 teaspoons of the dill as well as the beer, just until a smooth batter forms. Scatter the remaining ¼ cup of flour in a shallow dish and place the panko in a separate shallow dish.

When the oil is at temperature, dredge about one-quarter of the pickle slices in the flour and then, one at a time, dunk in the batter to coat, shaking off any excess. Press the battered pickle slices into the panko and then fry until golden brown, about 2 minutes, flipping once. Transfer the fried pickle slices to the wire rack and continue battering and frying until all of the pickles are crisp.

In a small bowl, stir together the mayonnaise, sour cream, lemon zest and juice, the remaining 2 teaspoons of dill, and a few dashes of hot sauce. Serve the deep-fried pickles immediately with the dip, for maximum crispiness.

Note:
If you want to use your own Spicy Dill Quickles (page 97) for this, make a batch with a field or English cucumber sliced into ¼-inch rounds.

Crispy Onion Rings

SNACKS, SIDES, SWEETS, AND SIPS · SERVES 3 TO 4

Canola oil, for deep-frying

1 large yellow onion

¾ cup all-purpose flour

¾ cup cornstarch

½ teaspoon kosher salt

¼ teaspoon black pepper

¼ teaspoon garlic powder

¼ teaspoon cayenne pepper

¾–1 cup light-flavored beer, such as pilsner or lager, cold

1 cup panko breadcrumbs

Back before I started working in food, I worked as an insurance broker and, in true office-culture form, my work wife, Alysha, and I had a weekly routine of heading to a local haunt for a pint and a talk/vent about our days. Nothing made the stress of the job melt away more than those hangouts over apple pilsners and the best darn onion rings I'd ever had. These perfectly crispy rings are dedicated to Alysha and to whoever helps make the stress of your job just a little more manageable.

Preheat your oven to 200°F and set a wire rack on a large baking sheet. Place the baking sheet in the warm oven.

Heat 2 inches of oil in a deep sauté pan or Dutch oven to 350°F. If you do not have a thermometer, heat the oil until it shimmers or the end of a wooden spoon causes bubbles to form when gently dipped into it.

While the oil comes up to temperature, cut the onions into ½-inch-thick slices and separate them into rings. In a large bowl, whisk together the flour, cornstarch, salt, pepper, garlic powder, and cayenne pepper. Add the onion slices and toss to coat. Remove the onion slices and set aside.

Whisk ¾ cup of beer into the flour mixture just until combined, adding more beer if needed to reach a pancake batter consistency. Scatter the panko into a shallow dish.

Dip the onions into the beer batter one at a time, then dredge in the panko to coat. Place them in the hot oil in batches of five or six and fry until golden brown and crispy, about 3 to 4 minutes, flipping halfway through and adjusting the heat if the onion rings are browning too quickly.

Transfer the onion rings to the baking sheet in the oven and sprinkle immediately with additional salt. Continue battering, dredging, frying, and seasoning until all of the onion rings are cooked.

Jane's Corn on the Cob with Corn Butter

SNACKS, SIDES, SWEETS, AND SIPS · SERVES 4 WITH LEFTOVER CORN BUTTER

6 ears corn, shucked

1 tablespoon + ½ cup butter

Kosher salt

½ cup milk

2 tablespoons sugar

Black pepper

How is it that a particular dish made by a particular person can consistently be the best ever? For me, corn on the cob made by our family friend Jane is one of those dishes. Adding sugar and a bit of milk to the water is her trick to make them perfectly sweet and crisp every single time. This little switch to the cooking liquid plus the addition of corn-infused butter makes for one heck of a summer side.

Remove the kernels from 2 of the ears of corn by standing them on their ends on a clean kitchen towel and running a knife down the sides.

Place a skillet over medium heat and melt in the 1 tablespoon of butter. Add the kernels and cook, stirring frequently, just until the corn begins to smell a little nutty and develop some color, 2 minutes. Transfer the corn to a food processor fitted with a steel blade and let cool to room temperature. When cool, add the ½ cup of butter, season well with salt, and process until smooth, scraping down the sides of the bowl a few times as you go. Transfer the corn butter to a serving dish and set aside.

Fill a large pot with water and set it to boil over high heat. When the water is boiling, stir in the milk, sugar, and 2 teaspoons of salt and add the remaining 4 ears of corn. Cover the pot with a tight-fitting lid, turn the heat down to medium, and allow the corn to cook just until the kernels are tender, 6 to 8 minutes.

Serve the hot corn slathered with the corn butter and sprinkled with extra salt and some pepper. Store any remaining corn butter covered in the fridge for up to 4 days.

Fried Squash Blossoms with Anchovy and Lemon

SNACKS, SIDES, SWEETS, AND SIPS · SERVES 4 TO 6

FOR THE BLOSSOMS AND FILLING

12 squash blossoms

Canola oil, for deep-frying

¾ cup ricotta cheese

½ cup finely grated Pecorino Romano cheese

2 anchovy fillets, very finely minced

1 garlic clove, very finely minced

1 lemon, zested

1 teaspoon lemon juice

2 teaspoons finely chopped flat-leaf parsley

1 teaspoon finely chopped chives

½ teaspoon crushed red pepper flakes

Kosher salt

FOR THE BATTER AND SERVING

½ cup all-purpose flour

2 tablespoons cornstarch

¾ teaspoon kosher salt

¾ cup soda water

4 handfuls arugula

1 tablespoon extra virgin olive oil

½ lemon

Flaky sea salt

Crushed red pepper flakes

I have a bit of a motto when it comes to the incredible bounty of summer vegetables and those fun, sometimes confounding, farmers' market finds: When in doubt, fry! And stuff with cheese and chopped up anchovies, if possible.

For the squash blossoms, carefully remove the pollen-covered stamens by breaking and pinching them out with your fingers, being careful not to rip too much of the blossom. Discard the stamens and set the blossoms aside.

In a deep sauté pan or a Dutch oven set over medium heat, warm 2 inches of oil to 350°F. If you do not have a thermometer, heat the oil until it shimmers or the end of a wooden spoon causes bubbles to form when gently dipped into it. Preheat your oven to 200°F and place a baking sheet lined with a wire rack on the middle rack.

While the oil heats, prepare the filling by mixing together the ricotta, Pecorino Romano, anchovies, garlic, lemon zest and juice, parsley, chives, and red pepper flakes. Season with salt and set aside.

For the batter, mix together the flour, cornstarch, and salt in a small bowl. Whisk in the soda water until combined. The batter should be completely smooth and quite thin so that it does not weigh down the delicate blossoms, but do not overmix.

Using a small spoon, gently fill each squash blossom with about 1 tablespoon of the filling mixture. Gently twist the tops of the squash blossoms to enclose the filling.

When the oil is at temperature, dip 4 of the stuffed blossoms into the batter and fry until golden all over, about 2 to 3 minutes, flipping once. Remove from the oil and transfer to the wire rack in the oven to keep warm while you continue battering and frying the rest of the blossoms.

Place the arugula on a serving dish and drizzle it with the oil. Transfer the fried blossoms to the arugula, grate over the lemon zest, squeeze on the juice, and season with flaky sea salt and red pepper flakes and serve immediately.

Cacio e Pepe Salad

SNACKS, SIDES, SWEETS, AND SIPS · SERVES 4

1 garlic clove, very finely minced

3 tablespoons lemon juice (1–2 lemons)

3 tablespoons mayonnaise

1 tablespoon extra virgin olive oil

2 teaspoons Dijon mustard

½–1 teaspoon black pepper, plus more for serving

¼ cup finely grated Parmigiano-Reggiano cheese, plus more for serving

2 tablespoons finely grated Pecorino Romano cheese, plus more for serving

Kosher salt

6 large handfuls baby kale or arugula

A cheese and pepper–heavy spin on Caesar salad? Yes, please, I would like that very much.

In a large serving bowl, whisk together the garlic and lemon juice. Set aside for a few minutes to allow the garlic to marinate in the juice. Add the mayonnaise, oil, and Dijon and whisk to combine. Whisk in ½ teaspoon of pepper and then the cheeses. If needed, season with salt and up to another ½ teaspoon of pepper.

When you're ready to serve, add the kale and toss to coat. Top with a good grating of more Parmigiano-Reggiano and Pecorino Romano and some more pepper.

Late-Summer Salad aka Cottage Fridge Cleanout

SNACKS, SIDES, SWEETS, AND SIPS · SERVES 4 TO 6

2 ears corn, shucked

2 teaspoons butter or olive oil

Kosher salt and black pepper

3 medium tomatoes

2 peaches

½ lemon, juiced

2 tablespoons extra virgin olive oil

1 tablespoon red wine vinegar

2 teaspoons grainy Dijon mustard

¼ cup roughly chopped flat-leaf parsley

2 tablespoons roughly chopped dill

2 tablespoons roughly chopped chives

2 tablespoons roughly torn basil

4½ oz soft goat cheese

Our last meals at the cottage are usually made up of whatever I can find in the fridge. A few ears of corn, some almost-overripe tomatoes and peaches, any and all herbs from our last trip to the wharf farmers' market, and whatever nubs of cheese are left in the drawer get tossed into a bowl with a vinegary dressing for a quick use-'em-up salad. This recipe is easy to adjust to use whatever you find in your crisper, but to me, it isn't complete without at least some summer corn and ripe tomatoes.

Place a large skillet over medium heat.

Using a sharp knife, remove the kernels from the corn cobs by standing them on their end on top of a clean kitchen towel and slicing down the sides.

Place the butter in the skillet along with the corn. Season with salt and pepper, and, stirring frequently, cook until golden, about 2 to 3 minutes. Transfer the cooked corn to a large bowl. Core the tomatoes, remove the pits from the peaches, slice each into eight wedges, and add them to the corn.

In a small bowl, whisk together the lemon juice, oil, vinegar, and Dijon. Pour this over the corn, tomatoes, and peaches and add the parsley, dill, chives, and basil. Season with salt and pepper and gently toss everything together. Set aside to allow the flavors to meld for 10 to 15 minutes, or cover and refrigerate overnight.

When you're ready to serve, crumble the goat cheese over top and season with a little more pepper.

Classic Ice Cream Sandwiches

FOR THE CAKE

½ cup butter, melted

½ cup sugar

1 egg

1 teaspoon vanilla extract

½ cup all-purpose flour

¼ cup Dutch process cocoa powder

½ teaspoon kosher salt

¼ teaspoon baking powder

FOR THE NO-CHURN ICE CREAM

1¼ cups sweetened condensed milk

1 teaspoon vanilla extract or ½ vanilla bean, scraped

¼ teaspoon kosher salt

2 cups whipping (35%) cream

If you ask me, the classic ice cream sandwich can only be made with thin, cake-like chocolate cookies and the fluffiest vanilla ice cream, one that would make Messrs. Ben and Jerry blush and protest.

Preheat your oven to 350°F. Grease two 9-inch square baking pans with cooking spray and line with a sling of parchment paper so that it covers the bottom and comes up two facing sides.

For the cake, in a mixing bowl, or a stand mixer fitted with a paddle attachment, beat together the melted butter, sugar, egg, and vanilla on medium-high speed until well combined and a little lighter in color, about 1 to 2 minutes. In a separate bowl, sift together the flour, cocoa powder, salt, and baking powder. Add the dry ingredients to the butter mixture and stir just until combined and the batter is smooth.

Divide the batter equally between the two pans and spread it evenly across the entire base of each pan. Bake until the center of the cookies spring back when touched and look slightly dull, 8 to 10 minutes. Remove the cookies from the oven and allow them to cool to room temperature before turning them out onto a work surface and peeling away the parchment.

Line one of the 9-inch square baking pans with plastic wrap so that it hangs over the edges and place one of the cookies in the bottom. Transfer this to the freezer to chill while you make the no-churn ice cream.

For the ice cream, whisk together the condensed milk, vanilla, and salt in a large bowl until well combined. In a separate bowl, or a stand mixer fitted with a whisk attachment, whip the cream until stiff peaks form, about 2 to 3 minutes. Using a rubber spatula, gently fold one-third of the whipped cream into the condensed milk mixture. Fold in the remaining cream in two additions and set aside.

Retrieve the cookie in its baking pan from the freezer. Pour the ice cream base over the cookie, spreading it into an even layer, and top with the other cookie. Gently fold the plastic wrap over top to cover and place in the freezer for at least 6 hours but preferably overnight.

When you're ready to serve, turn the ice cream sandwich out of the pan and, using a sharp knife, cut it into eight equal portions. Serve immediately or wrap each portion in plastic wrap or wax paper and store in the freezer for up to 2 weeks.

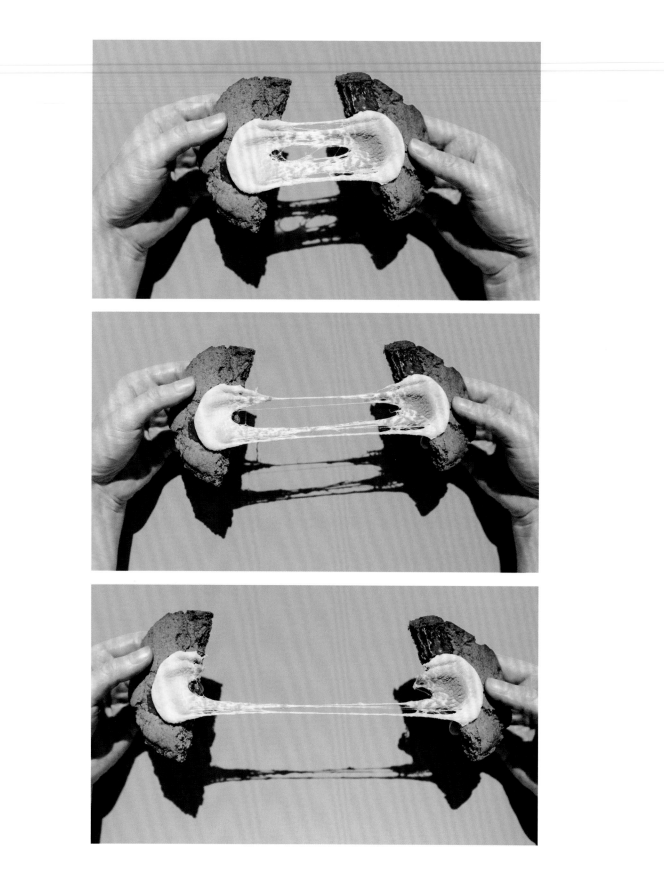

S'more Cookies

½ cup butter

½ cup packed brown sugar

½ cup sugar

1 egg

1 teaspoon vanilla extract

¾ cup graham cracker crumbs

¾ cup bread flour

½ cup all-purpose flour

2 teaspoons cornstarch

1½ teaspoons baking soda

½ teaspoon kosher salt

8 oz milk chocolate chunks

12 regular marshmallows

Regardless of their status as a summertime fireside staple, I am one of those people who has little to no patience when toasting marshmallows. After 20 seconds of attempting to slowly obtain that golden-brown exterior and perfectly gooey interior, I usually end up sticking my marshmallow directly in the flame and lighting it ablaze. These cookies remove the open flame from the s'mores equation without sacrificing flavor, therefore bringing the chance of me igniting anything down to between 0% and 5%.

Preheat your oven to 350°F and line two baking sheets with parchment paper.

In a mixing bowl, or a stand mixer fitted with a paddle attachment, beat the butter and both sugars on high speed until light and creamy, scraping down the bowl at least once midway through, about 3 to 4 minutes. Scrape down the bowl again, add the egg and vanilla, and then beat well until combined.

In a separate bowl, stir together the graham cracker crumbs, both flours, cornstarch, baking soda, and salt. Add the chocolate chunks and stir well to combine. Add the dry ingredients to the butter and sugar mixture and mix on low speed just until combined.

Using a 2 oz ice cream scoop or a large tablespoon, scoop six large cookies onto each prepared baking sheet. Bake the cookies a sheet at a time until their edges and top are set but they are still quite soft in the middle, 15 to 16 minutes. Cut a small piece off the side of each marshmallow to expose the sticky insides. Place a marshmallow, cut-side down, on the center of each cookie. Turn the broiler on to high until the marshmallows are lightly toasted, 1 to 2 minutes.

Allow the s'mores to cool on the baking sheet for 10 minutes, then transfer to a wire rack to cool. Bake the second sheet of cookies as you did the first and enjoy immediately or transfer to a resealable container and store at room temperature for up to 5 days.

Butter Tart Cupcakes

SNACKS, SIDES, SWEETS, AND SIPS · MAKES 18 CUPCAKES

FOR THE CUPCAKES

½ cup butter, room temperature

1 cup + 2 tablespoons packed dark brown sugar

2 eggs

¼ cup + 2 tablespoons milk

1 teaspoon white vinegar

1 teaspoon vanilla extract

½ teaspoon maple extract

1½ cups all-purpose flour

1 teaspoon baking powder

½ teaspoon kosher salt

FOR THE BUTTERCREAM

1 cup butter, room temperature

¼ cup + 2 tablespoons packed brown sugar

3 tablespoons pure maple syrup

2½ cups icing sugar

1½ tablespoons cream or milk

¾ teaspoon vanilla extract

¼ teaspoon maple extract

½ teaspoon kosher salt

FOR DECORATING

1 Pastry Sheet, baked (see below), or baked store-bought pie shell, broken into shards

½ cup chopped pecans (optional)

¼ cup chopped raisins (optional)

I'm pretty sure every Canadian has their favorite butter tart, and I'm no exception. Mine come from the wonderful ladies at the Tastefully Yours Baking stand at the Gravenhurst farmers' market. I cannot tell you how absolutely perfect they are. They are so perfect, in fact, that I rarely even try my hand at making my own butter tarts because I know that I'll never reach the lofty flavor peak their personal pies provide. But while I wouldn't ever dare try to replicate, I'm happy to let myself be inspired by those oozy tarts with these butter tart cupcakes that taste like pure summer to me.

Preheat your oven to 325°F, set out two muffin tins, and line 18 of the cavities with cupcake liners. Pour some water into the empty cavities to prevent burning.

In a mixing bowl, or a stand mixer fitted with a paddle attachment, cream the butter and sugar together on high speed, scraping down the bowl once or twice, until light and fluffy, about 2 to 3 minutes. Add the eggs one at a time, scraping down the bowl and beating well after each addition.

Combine the milk, vinegar, and both extracts in a glass measuring cup and set aside. In a separate bowl, sift together the flour, baking powder, and salt.

Add the dry ingredients to the butter mixture in three additions, mixing on low speed, alternating with two additions of the milk mixture. Scrape down the bowl with a rubber spatula and mix by hand just until fully combined.

Divide the mixture into the lined muffin tins using a 2 oz ice cream scoop or a large tablespoon and bake until lightly golden and a skewer inserted into the center of a cupcake comes out clean, 20 to 25 minutes. Allow the cupcakes to cool completely in the pan while you make the buttercream and decorations.

Pastry Sheet

¼ cup all-purpose flour
⅛ teaspoon kosher salt
2 tablespoons butter, cold
1 tablespoon ice water

Preheat the oven to 425°F and line a baking sheet with parchment paper.

In a small bowl, stir together the flour and salt and cut or snap in the butter until it resembles a coarse meal with pea-sized pieces of butter. Stir in the water and bring the dough together, adding more, about 1 teaspoon at a time, if needed. Turn the dough out onto the prepared baking sheet and roll it into a ¼-inch-thick sheet.

Bake the pastry sheet until golden brown and crisp, 10 to 12 minutes. Cool completely before breaking into pieces.

For the buttercream, cream the butter, brown sugar, and maple syrup together in a large bowl, or a stand mixer fitted with a paddle attachment, on high speed until light and fluffy, about 2 to 3 minutes. Slowly begin beating in the icing sugar, about ¼ cup at a time, until fully incorporated. Add the cream or milk, both extracts, and salt and beat on high speed until light and fluffy, about 1 to 2 minutes.

To decorate the cooled cupcakes, either spread the buttercream on with the back of a spoon or an offset spatula or pipe it on with a piping bag fitted with a decorative tip. Sprinkle the cupcakes with the broken-up pastry sheet and the chopped pecans and raisins (if using). Store leftover cupcakes in a resealable container at room temperature for up to 3 days.

Coconut Sour Cream Pie

SNACKS, SIDES, SWEETS, AND SIPS · MAKES 1 (9-INCH) DEEP DISH PIE

FOR THE CRUST

½ cup coconut oil

2 cups all-purpose flour

1 tablespoon sugar

½ teaspoon kosher salt

½ cup butter, cold, cut into pats

1 egg

2–3 tablespoons milk, cold

FOR THE FILLING

1¼ cups sweetened condensed milk

1 (14 oz) can coconut milk

½ cup sour cream

6 egg yolks

1 cup sweetened shredded coconut

½ teaspoon kosher salt

½ teaspoon coconut extract

FOR THE TOPPING

2 cups whipping (35%) cream

½ cup sour cream

½ teaspoon coconut extract

¼ cup icing sugar

¼ cup large-flaked sweetened coconut, toasted

There are a few ingredients that can take a dessert from good to great. They're usually ones that, upon first glance, warrant a double take. (For instance, how in the world does sour cream work in a coconut cream pie?) Well, for me, it's how those ingredients offer a counterbalance to the dominant flavor that really make a sweet dish sing. Think of flaky salt on chocolate chip cookies. The sour cream in this recipe helps brighten what could otherwise be a cloyingly sweet pie and turns it into a perfect version instead.

For the crust, line a small baking sheet with parchment paper. Spoon the solid coconut oil onto the parchment paper and spread it into a roughly ¼-inch-thick layer. Place the pan in your freezer for 15 to 20 minutes to chill and firm up the oil.

Place the flour, sugar, and salt in a food processor fitted with a steel blade and pulse two to three times to combine. Add the butter and pulse five to six times, or until the butter is broken into pea-sized pieces.

In a small bowl, whisk together the egg and 2 tablespoons of the milk and set aside. Remove the coconut oil from the freezer, cut or break it into roughly 1-inch pieces, and add to the food processor. Pulse two to three times, just until the coconut oil pieces are about the same size as the butter pieces. Pour in the egg mixture, pulsing just until incorporated and the dough holds together when squeezed. If the mixture is dry, add the remaining 1 tablespoon of milk, 1 teaspoon at a time.

Transfer the dough to a piece of plastic wrap and form it into a flat disk. Wrap it well and refrigerate for at least 1 hour, or up to 2 days.

Remove the pie dough from the fridge and allow it to sit at room temperature for a few minutes before rolling. Roll out the dough on a lightly floured work surface to about ¼-inch thick, then transfer it to a deep 9-inch pie plate and trim and crimp the edges. Chill the crust for 30 minutes, then dock the bottom of it by poking it about a dozen times with a fork. Preheat your oven to 400°F. Line the chilled and docked crust with parchment paper or aluminum foil and fill it with pie weights

CONTINUES

or dried beans. Blind-bake the crust until the edges are golden, 18 to 20 minutes, then remove the foil or parchment and pie weights, and continue to bake the crust until the base is golden brown, about 8 minutes. Turn the oven down to 325°F, remove the crust, and let cool completely to room temperature, then place the cooled pie shell on a baking sheet.

For the filling, in a large bowl, whisk together the condensed milk, coconut milk, sour cream, and egg yolks until smooth. Whisk in the shredded coconut, salt, and coconut extract. Pour the mixture into the pie shell. Bake until set but still slightly jiggly in the center, 50 minutes to 1 hour.

Remove the pie from the oven and allow to cool at room temperature for 2 hours. Cover lightly with plastic wrap and transfer the pie to the fridge to chill completely for at least 3 hours, or up to overnight.

When the pie is chilled, prepare the topping. Place the cream, sour cream, coconut extract, and icing sugar in a mixing bowl, or a stand mixer fitted with a whisk attachment, and whip on high speed until stiff peaks form, about 2 to 3 minutes.

Dollop the whipped cream mixture on top of the chilled pie and finish with the toasted coconut. Store any leftover pie covered in the fridge for up to 4 days.

Blueberry Lavender Oat Tart

SNACKS, SIDES, SWEETS, AND SIPS · MAKES 1 (9- OR 10-INCH) TART

1½ pints fresh blueberries

½ cup sugar

1½ teaspoons cornstarch

¾ teaspoon dried food-grade lavender

½ lemon, zested and juiced

1 teaspoon almond extract, divided

¾ cup butter, room temperature

¼ cup packed dark brown sugar

½ cup sugar

1 egg

1 cup rolled oats

1 cup whole wheat flour

½ teaspoon baking powder

½ teaspoon kosher salt

½ teaspoon ground cardamom

½ teaspoon ground cinnamon

⅛ teaspoon freshly grated nutmeg

1 tablespoon sliced almonds

Vanilla skyr or Greek yogurt, for serving

Note:

The blueberry filling can be made up to 2 weeks in advance and stored in the fridge. Also, I wouldn't blame you if some of it made its way onto your next cheeseboard.

Almost like a cross between a blueberry pie and a date square, this tart is the perfect thing to bring to a summer cookout. It's not at all fussy and the whole wheat crust gives this dessert a healthy spin, making leftovers perfect for breakfast the next morning.

Preheat your oven to 350°F and lightly grease a 9- or 10-inch cake pan or removable-bottom tart pan with cooking spray.

In a small saucepan, stir together the blueberries, sugar, cornstarch, and lavender, then add the lemon zest and juice and ½ teaspoon of the almond extract. Place over medium heat and simmer until the fruit has broken down and the mixture is thick and jammy, 15 to 20 minutes. Set aside to cool slightly.

In a mixing bowl, or a stand mixer fitted with a paddle attachment, beat together the butter and both sugars on high speed until well combined. Beat in the egg and the remaining ½ teaspoon of almond extract and set aside.

Place the oats in a food processor fitted with a steel blade and pulse until finely ground, about eight to ten pulses. Add the flour, baking powder, salt, cardamom, cinnamon, and nutmeg and pulse to combine. Add the dry ingredients to the butter mixture and mix on low speed just until combined.

Transfer about three-quarters of the dough mixture to the prepared pan and, using your hands or a rubber spatula, spread and press the mixture into the bottom of the pan and slightly up the sides to form a ½-inch-high or so crust. Spoon the blueberry mixture into the center of the crust and carefully spread it into an even layer, making sure to keep the filling within the crust. Tear and dollop the remaining dough over top of the filling, scatter on the almonds, and place the pan on a baking sheet in case it bubbles over in the oven.

Bake until golden brown, 35 to 40 minutes. The filling might be quite fluid at this point but it will set up upon cooling. Allow the tart to cool to room temperature and serve topped with a spoonful of yogurt.

Vanilla Almond Chiffon Cake with Wine-Soaked Strawberries

SNACKS, SIDES, SWEETS, AND SIPS · MAKES 1 TUBE CAKE

FOR THE CAKE

7 eggs, separated

½ teaspoon cream of tartar (see note)

1½ cups sugar, divided

⅓ cup vegetable oil

½ cup milk

1 teaspoon vanilla extract

1 teaspoon almond extract

1½ cups all-purpose flour

2 teaspoons baking powder

½ teaspoon kosher salt

FOR THE STRAWBERRIES

4 cups quartered fresh strawberries

½ cup dry red wine, such as Pinot Noir

¼ cup sugar

½ teaspoon vanilla extract

Sweetened whipped cream, for serving

A chiffon cake relies mainly on whipped egg whites for its rise and volume but has the helpful addition of baking powder to assist with stability and egg yolks and oil to amp up the flavor and texture. The trickiest part of any recipe that uses egg whites as a leavener is the process of folding, but have no fear. As the eternally wise Moira Rose once said with respect to the method: "You fold it in. . . You just . . . here's what you do. You just fold it in."

Preheat your oven to 325°F and place an ungreased removable-bottom tube pan on a large baking sheet.

For the cake, place the egg whites and cream of tartar in a stand mixer fitted with a whisk attachment or in a large glass or metal bowl paired with a hand mixer and whip on high speed until soft peaks form, about 1 to 2 minutes. With the mixer running, slowly sprinkle in ¾ cup of the sugar. Continue to whip just until the whites reach stiff peaks, about 2 to 3 minutes, and set aside.

In a clean bowl of your stand mixer fitted with a whisk attachment or in a separate bowl paired with your hand mixer, whip together the yolks and remaining ¾ cup sugar on high speed until light and almost doubled in volume, about 2 to 3 minutes. With the mixer running on low speed, slowly stream in the oil, mixing until fully incorporated. Add the milk and both extracts and whip just until combined.

Remove the bowl from its stand and sift in the flour, baking powder, and salt. Using a rubber spatula, fold in the dry ingredients by cutting through the center of the batter and scooping and folding it over onto itself until fully combined. Gently add about one-third of the whipped egg whites to the bowl and fold them in until almost combined. Fold in the remaining egg whites in two additions, being careful not to overmix and deflate the egg whites.

Gently transfer the cake batter to the ungreased tube pan and bake without opening the oven door for 45 minutes. Turn the heat up to 350°F and bake until the cake is golden brown and a skewer inserted into the center comes out clean, another 10 to 15 minutes.

Place the neck of a glass bottle such as an empty wine bottle in the center of the tube pan and flip it over so that the cake cools fully to room temperature as it hangs upside down. This will take about 3 hours.

While the cake cools, combine the strawberries with the wine and sugar in a nonreactive bowl. Stir well, cover, and place in the fridge to macerate for at least 2 hours, or up to overnight.

When the cake has cooled, run a thin knife around the outside edge to loosen it from the pan. Remove the cake from the outside pan and use the knife to loosen the bottom and center of the cake from the tube portion of the pan. Carefully turn the cake off the tube and onto a serving plate, slice, and serve with the macerated strawberries and a dollop of sweetened whipped cream. The untopped cake will keep well at room temperature, wrapped in plastic, for up to 5 days.

Note:
If you don't have cream of tartar, ¼ teaspoon of white vinegar or lemon juice will also work.

Neapolitan Ice Cream Cake

SNACKS, SIDES, SWEETS, AND SIPS · MAKES 1 (9-INCH SQUARE) CAKE

¾ cup all-purpose flour

½ cup sugar

¼ cup Dutch process cocoa powder

1 teaspoon baking soda

¼ teaspoon baking powder

¼ teaspoon kosher salt

¼ cup buttermilk

3 tablespoons canola oil

1 egg

1 teaspoon vanilla extract, divided

¼ cup hot coffee

1 quart strawberry ice cream

2 cups whipping (35%) cream

3 tablespoons icing sugar

2 waffle or sugar cones, roughly broken

1 tablespoon rainbow sprinkles

I think we can all agree that Neapolitan ice cream is the people's ice cream. Maybe it's not your all-time favorite flavor but there is something for everyone in the mix. Vanilla for the refined palate, chocolate for the kid at heart, and strawberry for those who, like me, love a fruity dessert. This ice cream cake brings all the classic flavors of a Neapolitan ice cream cone together into one party-worthy slice.

Preheat your oven to 350°F. Spray a 9-inch square baking pan with cooking spray and line with a sling of parchment paper so that it covers the bottom and comes up two facing sides.

In a large bowl, sift together the flour, sugar, cocoa powder, baking soda, baking powder, and salt and make a well in the center. Whisk in the buttermilk, oil, egg, and ½ teaspoon of vanilla just until combined, then whisk in the hot coffee. The batter will be pretty thin, but that's what you're looking for.

Pour the batter into the prepared cake pan and bake until a skewer inserted into the center of the cake comes out clean, 20 to 25 minutes. Allow the cake to cool completely in the pan, then place in the freezer to firm up and freeze slightly, 1 to 2 hours.

If you're using strawberry ice cream from a box rather than a tub, simply open the box and cut the ice cream into about 1-inch-thick slices and arrange on top of the cold cake so that it covers the whole surface. If you're using a tub of ice cream, place it in the fridge for 30 minutes to 1 hour, just until softened slightly, then scoop it onto the cake and spread it into an even layer. Place the ice cream–topped cake back in the freezer to firm up.

Place the whipping cream, icing sugar, and remaining ½ teaspoon of vanilla in a mixing bowl, or a stand mixer fitted with a whisk attachment, and whip on high speed just until stiff peaks form, about 2 minutes.

Spread the whipped cream over the ice cream layer and scatter the broken sugar or waffle cones over the top. Sprinkle with the rainbow sprinkles and then return the cake to the freezer for at least 30 minutes to chill.

To serve, lift the cake out of the pan using the overhanging parchment and slice with a clean warm knife. Store any remaining cake tightly covered in the freezer for up to 1 week.

Peach Tarragon Frauvy B.

SNACKS, SIDES, SWEETS, AND SIPS · MAKES 6 COCKTAILS

1 (750 ml) bottle Sauvignon Blanc

1½ cups peach juice

¼ cup elderflower liqueur

¼ cup lemon juice

4 very ripe peaches, peeled and roughly chopped

1 tablespoon finely chopped tarragon

Tarragon sprigs, for garnish

Peach wedges, for garnish

Remember back in 2016 and 2017 when it seemed like the whole world went bonkers for frosé? I totally get it. It is super delicious and the perfect summer beverage, but lately I got to thinking about all the other wines that could work for a boozy slushie. This fun cocktail is the perfect way to use up soft peaches, and it all starts with a budget-friendly bottle of Sauvignon Blanc.

Pour the Sauvignon Blanc, peach juice, and elderflower liqueur into a 9- × 13-inch baking pan, stir to combine, and place in the freezer overnight.

When you're ready to serve, scrape the frozen wine mixture into a blender and add the lemon juice, peaches, and tarragon and blend until smooth.

Serve immediately in glasses garnished with a sprig of tarragon and wedge of peach.

If you have any slushie left over, place the blender back in the freezer for up to 30 minutes at a time, blending after each 30-minute period and again before serving.

Note:
Freezing wine tends to dull any nuanced flavors it has, so feel free to use a cheaper bottle of Sauvignon Blanc for this recipe.

Kind of a Big Dill

1½ oz gin

½ oz elderflower liqueur

1 oz lemon juice

2 (1-inch-thick) slices cucumber, divided

1 sprig dill, plus extra for garnish

Ice cubes

2 oz sparkling water

When giant bunches of dill start to pop up at fruit shops and farmers' markets, I take that as a sure sign of summer. It's one of those herbs that seems to only come in handfuls big enough to feed an army and it can sometimes get a little tricky to think of new ways to enjoy it. This pun-tastic cocktail is here to help with the sweet floral flavors of gin and elderflower and a bit of a nod to my favorite crunchable, the dill pickle.

In a cocktail shaker, combine the gin, elderflower liqueur, and lemon juice. Roughly chop 1 slice of the cucumber and add it to the shaker along with the dill. Using a wooden spoon or a cocktail muddler, muddle well to break down the cucumber and dill.

Fill the shaker about halfway with ice cubes, cover with the lid, and shake for 20 seconds to chill very well.

Strain the cocktail into a coupe, top with sparkling water and garnish with the remaining cucumber slice and some dill.

Grilled Caesars

SNACKS, SIDES, SWEETS, AND SIPS · MAKES 5 COCKTAILS

2½ lb ripe tomatoes, halved

¼ yellow onion

3 limes, halved

7 celery stalks, divided

2 tablespoons sugar

½ teaspoon celery salt

¼ teaspoon black pepper

1 cup bottled clam juice

1–2 tablespoons prepared horseradish

10–12 dashes Worcestershire sauce

8–10 dashes hot sauce

7½ oz vodka or gin, chilled

2 tablespoons Montreal steak spice

Ice cubes

Did anyone else have friends in university whose bar drink was a Bloody Caesar? Those people have one of those chaotic personalities I will never understand. To me, a Caesar should be enjoyed outside on a sunny summer day with, or preferably containing, the smoky flavor of the grill.

Preheat your grill to high. Place the tomatoes, onion, and limes on a vegetable grilling tray. Roughly chop 2 stalks of the celery into 1-inch pieces, add them to the tray, and place it on the preheated grill. Cook, turning the veg occasionally, until well charred, about 4 to 6 minutes.

Set the charred lime halves aside and carefully transfer the charred vegetables to a blender. Squeeze in the juice of 2 lime halves, add in the sugar, celery salt, pepper, and clam juice, and season to taste with horseradish, Worcestershire, and hot sauce. Blend on high until smooth.

Strain this mixture through a fine mesh sieve into a serving jug and place in the fridge to chill for at least 1 hour, or up to 4 days.

When you're ready to serve, stir in the booze and prepare the glasses by juicing 2 of the grilled lime halves into a shallow dish. Cut the remaining lime halves into wedges for a garnish. In a separate shallow dish, sprinkle in the Montreal steak spice. Dip the rim of five glasses into the lime juice, then into the steak spice, and fill each glass with ice cubes. Pour the cocktail mixture over the ice and garnish with a wedge of grilled lime and a celery stalk.

Autumn
Cozy, Hearty, and Nostalgic

Almond Butter and Jam Waffles

BREAKFAST THROUGH DINNER · MAKES 8 LARGE WAFFLES

FOR THE WAFFLES

2 cups all-purpose flour

½ cup almond flour

¼ cup sugar

1 tablespoon baking powder

1 teaspoon baking soda

½ teaspoon kosher salt

2 cups buttermilk

¼ cup butter, melted

2 eggs, separated

1 teaspoon vanilla extract

½ teaspoon almond extract

FOR TOPPING

¼ cup sliced almonds

½ cup prepared Concord grape jam

1 cup Concord grapes

½–1 cup almond butter

2–4 tablespoons honey

Note:

If you can't find Concord grapes, feel free to leave them out and just use double the amount of jam.

I've always been a bit of a Jim Halpert when it comes to early-in-the-day foods. For anyone who hasn't watched *The Office*, what I mean is that I'm a true creature of habit, but rather than Jim's classic ham and cheese or occasional "big tuna," my go-to morning toast or brown-bag lunch usually involves nut butter and jam. I won't get into my thoughts on PB&J (Pam Beesly and Jim), but these fancied-up AB&J waffles are guaranteed to get you an invite to the Finer Things Club.

Preheat your oven to 200°F and place a baking sheet lined with a wire rack inside.

For the waffles, in a large bowl, whisk together both flours, sugar, baking powder, baking soda, and salt. Pour in the buttermilk and melted butter, add the egg yolks and both extracts, and whisk just to combine. Set the mixture aside for 10 minutes.

Meanwhile, preheat your waffle iron according to the manufacturer's instructions.

Using a hand mixer, whip the egg whites on high speed until stiff peaks form, about 2 to 3 minutes. Using a spatula, fold the egg whites into the batter in two additions. Be careful not to overmix.

When the waffle iron is at temperature, grease it with cooking spray and pour about ½ cup of batter into each waffle well. Cook until crisp and golden brown, about 3 to 5 minutes, depending on your waffle iron. Transfer the cooked waffles to the warm oven, then continue with the rest of the batter.

For the topping, in a small pan, toast the sliced almonds over medium heat until golden and fragrant, about 2 minutes, stirring occasionally, and set aside. Heat the jam in a small saucepan over low heat or in the microwave just until warm, then stir in the grapes.

To serve, dot the waffles with almond butter, spoon over some of the grape mixture, scatter over the toasted almonds, and add a little honey to taste. Any leftover waffles can be stacked, separated by a small square of parchment paper, and frozen in a large freezer bag. To reheat, simply toast until hot and crisp.

Bourbon Pecan BLT

BREAKFAST THROUGH DINNER · SERVES 2

6 slices thick-cut bacon

2 tablespoons maple syrup

1 tablespoon bourbon

1 tablespoon finely chopped pecans

¼ teaspoon black pepper

3 tablespoons mayonnaise

1 tablespoon finely chopped chives

4 slices sourdough or whole grain bread, toasted

2–4 leaves Bibb lettuce

1 ripe tomato, sliced

3½ oz smoked cheddar cheese, sliced

2 teaspoons grainy Dijon mustard

½ ripe avocado

Kosher salt

Perhaps it's due to the woody, fiery smell of fallen leaves reminding me of smoky bourbon and pecans, but the warmth and bounty of Southern flavors always seem to creep into my kitchen as the leaves start to turn. Infusing these Southern staples into one of Aaron's favorite sandwiches makes for a pretty darn great BLT.

Line a baking sheet with parchment paper and set aside.

Lay the bacon in a cold nonstick skillet and place it over medium heat. Cook the bacon just until lightly caramelized on both sides and still chewy, about 4 minutes per side.

In a small bowl, mix together the maple syrup, bourbon, pecans, and pepper and spoon some over the bacon. Continue cooking the bacon, flipping frequently and applying more of the pecan mixture as you go, until the bacon is crisp, about 2 more minutes. Transfer the bacon to the prepared baking sheet and set aside.

In a small bowl, combine the mayonnaise, chives, and any remaining pecan mixture and whisk together.

To assemble the sandwiches, divide the mayonnaise mixture between 2 slices of toast and spread into an even layer. Layer on the lettuce, tomato, bacon, and cheese. Spread the Dijon over the remaining 2 slices of toast and mash on the avocado. Season with salt and pepper, top with the avocado toast to sandwich, slice diagonally, and serve.

Spanakopita Grilled Cheese

BREAKFAST THROUGH DINNER · SERVES 2

3 tablespoons butter, divided

½ shallot, finely minced

Kosher salt and black pepper

1 garlic clove, finely minced

2 large handfuls baby spinach

2 tablespoons brick-style cream cheese

½ lemon, zested and juiced

¼ cup crumbled feta cheese

2 teaspoons finely chopped dill

1 teaspoon finely chopped flat-leaf parsley

¼ teaspoon crushed red pepper flakes

4 slices sourdough bread

½ cup grated mozzarella or fontina cheese

This sandwich is somehow simultaneously healthier and more chock-full of cheese than any grilled cheese sandwich I've ever had. It's like a cross between the classic golden-brown sandwich, crispy spanakopita, and spinach dip, and I can think of few things I'd rather dig into on a crisp autumn afternoon.

Place a large nonstick skillet over medium heat and melt 1 tablespoon of the butter. Add the shallots and season with salt and pepper. Cook the shallots until translucent and just starting to turn golden brown, about 2 minutes, then add the garlic and cook for an additional 30 seconds. Stir in the spinach and allow it to wilt down for 1 to 2 minutes.

When the spinach has wilted, add the cream cheese and lemon zest and juice, stirring until the cream cheese has melted. Remove the pan from the heat and stir in the feta, dill, parsley, and red pepper flakes. Season with salt and pepper. Transfer the spinach mixture to a bowl and set aside.

Using paper towel, wipe out the skillet and place it back on the heat.

Spread the remaining 2 tablespoons of butter over one side of each piece of bread. Place 2 of the slices, butter-side down, in the pan and scatter the mozzarella over each. Divide the spinach mixture over the cheese and spread it into an even layer so that it reaches the edges of the bread. Place the remaining pieces of bread, butter-side up, on top and press down the sandwiches with a spatula.

Cook each sandwich, flipping once, until the cheese has melted and the exterior is crisp and golden brown, 3 to 5 minutes per side.

Mushrooms and White Beans on Toast

BREAKFAST THROUGH DINNER · SERVES 2

3 tablespoons butter, divided

2 thick slices of bread

1 garlic clove, halved

2 large handfuls mixed mushrooms

2 teaspoons olive oil

Kosher salt and black pepper

1 cup canned or cooked white kidney beans (see note)

1½ cups chicken or vegetable broth

¼ cup chopped herbs, such as dill, flat-leaf parsley, oregano, sage, and/or thyme

2–4 tablespoons crumbled or grated cheese, such as goat cheese, feta, or Parmigiano-Reggiano

Red pepper flakes (optional)

Extra virgin olive oil

This is one of those chameleon recipes that can take you from breakfast and brunch all the way through to lunch and dinner. So much more than the sum of its parts, this pantry and fridge staple-based dish carries my husband and me through our busiest times.

Heat a large skillet or sauté pan over medium heat.

Spread 2 tablespoons of the butter over both pieces of bread, making sure to evenly coat both sides. Toast the bread in the hot pan until golden brown on both sides, 2 to 3 minutes per side. Transfer the toast to two shallow bowls or rimmed dinner plates and, while still hot from the pan, rub one or both sides of the toast with a cut side of the garlic clove. Then mince the garlic and set aside.

Turn the heat up to medium-high. Cut or tear your mushrooms into bite-sized pieces. Add the remaining 1 tablespoon of butter to the skillet along with the oil and then the mushrooms. Season with salt and pepper and cook, stirring occasionally and turning the heat down if the butter starts to burn, until the mushrooms are golden brown, about 2 minutes. Add the minced garlic and cook for an additional minute. Divide the mushrooms over the toasts and set the pan back onto the heat.

Add the beans to the hot pan along with the broth. Allow this to cook for about 1 minute, just to heat the beans and broth. Stir in the herbs, then spoon the mixture over the toast and mushrooms. Scatter the cheese over top and season with salt, some red pepper flakes (if using) and a drizzle of extra virgin olive oil.

Note:
To cook white kidney beans, cover 1 cup of dried beans with 4 inches of water and allow to soak at room temperature overnight. Drain the beans, transfer to a saucepan, and cover with a few inches of water. Flavor with aromatics, if desired, bring to a boil over medium-high heat, then reduce to low and simmer until tender, 1 to 1½ hours. Drain and season well with salt. This makes about 3 cups of cooked beans. Leftovers can be stored in a container in the fridge for up to 5 days.

Technically from a Can Tomato Soup with Savory Cheesy Churros

BREAKFAST THROUGH DINNER · SERVES 4 TO 5

FOR THE SOUP

1 (28 oz) can whole or diced tomatoes

4 garlic cloves, unpeeled

2 small shallots, roughly chopped

5–7 sprigs thyme

2 teaspoons sugar

Kosher salt and black pepper

1 tablespoon olive oil

1 tablespoon balsamic vinegar

2–3 cups low-sodium vegetable or chicken broth

1 tablespoon tomato paste

Lemon juice or balsamic vinegar

FOR THE CHURROS

2 teaspoons sugar

1½ tablespoons butter

½ teaspoon kosher salt

¼ teaspoon black pepper

1 cup all-purpose flour

Canola oil, for deep-frying

¼ cup ground Parmigiano-Reggiano cheese (see page 85), plus more for serving

1 tablespoon finely chopped flat-leaf parsley, plus more for serving

2 teaspoons finely chopped thyme, plus more for serving

1 egg yolk

We were never really a "tomato soup from the can" family when I was growing up. Instead, we liked the almost neon yellow chicken noodle soup from a sachet as an accompaniment to our grilled cheese. To me, canned tomato soup has always tasted oddly sweet, and the color was never quite right, so I set out to make my own version of smooth tomato soup that does, in fact, still start with a can.

Preheat your oven to 375°F.

For the soup, toss together the tomatoes and their juices, garlic, shallots, and thyme on a large baking sheet. Season the tomatoes with the sugar and some salt and pepper and drizzle with the oil and balsamic. Toss to combine and then roast, stirring occasionally, until the shallots are golden, the garlic is soft, and the tomato mixture is thickened, 35 to 40 minutes.

Meanwhile, heat 2 cups of the broth in a large pot over medium-low heat. When the vegetables are done, pick out the sprigs of thyme, carefully squash the roasted garlic out of its skin, discard the skin, and transfer the roasted tomatoes, shallots, and garlic to the pot of broth, along with the tomato paste. Using an immersion or stand blender (you may have to work in batches), blend the soup until smooth, adding more broth if needed. Taste the soup and season with salt, pepper, and a little lemon juice or balsamic to taste. Cover and keep warm over low heat, stirring occasionally.

For the churros, combine 1 cup of water with the sugar, butter, salt, and pepper in a small saucepan over medium heat. Bring to a boil, then add the flour all at once. Immediately stir the mixture with a wooden spoon until it forms a ball and a film is left on the bottom of the pan. Remove the pan from the heat and continue to stir for about 30 seconds.

Allow the dough to cool slightly while you heat about 3 inches of oil in a Dutch oven to 375°F. If you do not have a thermometer, heat the oil until it shimmers and the end of a wooden spoon causes bubbles to form when gently dipped into it.

When the dough is cooled slightly, beat in the Parmigiano-Reggiano, parsley, thyme, and egg yolk. Spoon the dough into a piping bag fitted with a large star tip and pipe 4- to 5-inch-long churros into the hot oil, using scissors to cut the dough as you go. Fry until golden, turning occasionally, 3 minutes. Transfer to a plate lined with paper towel to cool slightly.

Scatter the hot churros with ground Parmigiano-Reggiano, parsley, and thyme and serve alongside the soup for dunking.

Beer-Braised Brats with Pretzel Buns

BREAKFAST THROUGH DINNER · SERVES 6

FOR THE PRETZEL BUNS

2½ cups bread flour, plus more for kneading

2 teaspoons instant yeast

1 teaspoon salt

⅔ cup milk

2 tablespoons honey

2 tablespoons butter

¼ cup baking soda

1 egg

Flaky sea salt

FOR THE BRATS

1 small yellow onion, thickly sliced

2 garlic cloves, smashed

2 tablespoons Dijon mustard

½ teaspoon kosher salt

½ teaspoon black pepper

1 (16 oz) can lager

6 bratwursts

Prepared sauerkraut

Spicy or Dijon mustard

I've never been much of a souvenir buyer when traveling, opting instead to spend my time hunting down every single thing I want to eat. But on a high school trip across France and Germany, I happened across a vintage clothing store in Munich that I just had to stop in. Fast-forward to that evening, when I marched into the Hofbräuhaus beer hall adorned in my new-to-me dirndl and, not being old enough to drink back home and a life-long rule follower, I took a seat at a banquet table and happily nibbled away all night on a truly massive pretzel as everyone around me grew glassy-eyed.

For the buns, in a mixing bowl, or a stand mixer fitted with a dough hook attachment, combine the flour, yeast, and salt. In a microwave-safe dish or a small saucepan, combine the milk, honey, and butter with ⅓ cup of water and heat in the microwave or over low heat, just until the butter has melted and the mixture is slightly above body temperature. Pour the wet ingredients into the dry and stir with a wooden spoon just until a shaggy dough forms. Turn the dough out onto a well-floured work surface and knead until smooth and elastic, about 5 minutes.

Transfer the dough to a lightly greased bowl, cover with plastic wrap or a dinner plate, and set it in a warm spot to rise until doubled in volume, about 1½ hours. Meanwhile, line a large baking sheet with parchment paper and spray with cooking spray.

Punch down the dough, divide it into six equal pieces, and roll each piece into a 6-inch cylinder. Press down the tops of the buns to flatten them slightly, then place on the prepared baking sheet. Lightly drape a clean kitchen towel over the buns and place the pan back in a warm spot to rise until the buns are puffy and almost doubled in size, 30 to 40 minutes.

Preheat the oven to 400°F.

Combine 5 cups of water with the baking soda in a large sauté pan or saucepan set over medium-high heat. Give the mixture a stir and bring to a boil. Gently lower 3 of the buns into the water and allow them to poach for about 30 seconds, flipping once halfway through. Return the buns to the prepared baking sheet and poach the remaining buns.

Note:

If you like grilled onions on your sausages, remove the sliced onions from the liquid after poaching the sausages and place on your grill. Cook, flipping occasionally, until slightly charred, then transfer to a serving dish.

In a small bowl, whisk the egg with 1 tablespoon of water to make an egg wash and lightly brush it over the buns. Sprinkle with flaky sea salt and bake for 18 to 20 minutes until dark golden brown, with an internal temperature of 190°F. Remove the buns to a wire rack to cool completely.

For the brats, set a cast iron skillet on your grill and add the onions, garlic, Dijon, salt, and pepper. Carefully pour in the lager and turn the heat on to medium. Close the lid of the grill and bring the mixture to a simmer. Once simmering, nestle in the bratwursts, close the lid, and allow the sausages to poach for 5 to 6 minutes, flipping halfway through. You want them about halfway cooked.

Remove the sausages from the poaching liquid and cook directly on the grill until the casings are crisp and browned and the sausages have an internal temperature of 160°F, about 4 to 5 minutes per side. Allow the sausages to rest for 5 minutes before serving on the pretzel buns with sauerkraut and mustard.

My Favorite Delivery

FOR THE PIZZA DOUGH

2¼–2¾ cups bread flour

2 tablespoons milk powder

1½ teaspoons instant yeast

1¼ teaspoons sugar

1 teaspoon kosher salt

¼ cup butter, melted

3–4 tablespoons olive oil

FOR THE SAUCE AND TOPPINGS

1 cup canned whole tomatoes, drained, juice reserved

1 garlic clove, thinly sliced

1 tablespoon tomato paste

2 teaspoons olive oil

Kosher salt

Crushed red pepper flakes

2 teaspoons finely chopped flat-leaf parsley

2 teaspoons finely chopped basil

1 teaspoon finely chopped oregano

2–2½ cups grated mozzarella cheese

Thin-crust fancy pizza is all well and good, but when I'm craving a perfect cheesy delivery pie, pan pizza is the way to go. Feel free to top this baby with whatever you like (we're fans of the salty/sweet/spicy combo of green olives, pineapple, and pickled peppers), but be sure to cover the whole thing in shredded mozzarella from edge to edge for that signature crispy crust.

For the dough, in a mixing bowl, or a stand mixer fitted with a dough hook attachment, combine 2¼ cups of bread flour with the milk powder, yeast, sugar, and salt. Make a well in the center and add the melted butter as well as ¾ cup plus 2 tablespoons of warm tap water. Stir the mixture by hand until a shaggy dough forms, then knead on low speed until the dough forms a ball and is soft and springy, 5 to 6 minutes, adding more flour as needed, about ¼ cup at a time.

Transfer the dough to a lightly greased bowl, cover with plastic wrap or a dinner plate, and set in a warm spot until doubled in size, 1 to 1½ hours.

Meanwhile, prepare the sauce by combining the tomatoes with the garlic, tomato paste, and oil. Season with salt and red pepper flakes and, with clean hands, carefully squeeze the tomatoes to break them up and mix everything together. If the sauce is a little thick, thin it out with some of the reserved juice from the canned tomatoes, as the sauce will thicken further as it cooks in the oven. Stir in the parsley, basil, and oregano and set aside.

Place an oven rack in the bottom third of your oven, place a 10-inch cast iron skillet on the rack, and preheat the oven to 500°F.

When the dough has risen, punch it down and turn it out onto a lightly floured work surface. Flatten and stretch the dough into about a 10-inch circle and retrieve the hot cast iron skillet from the oven (remember those oven mitts!). Add 3 to 4 tablespoons of oil to the pan and carefully add the pizza dough. Top the dough with the prepared sauce, spreading it almost all the way to the edge, and scatter the mozzarella cheese over the entire surface. Add any toppings now as well.

Bake the pizza until the crust is golden brown and the cheese is bubbly and burnished, 18 to 20 minutes. Allow the pizza to cool slightly before slicing and serving.

Note:

If you're serving more than two or three people, double the recipe and use either two cast iron skillets or two (9- or 10-inch) round cake pans. You can also make a larger, thinner-crust pizza by pressing the dough into a 9- × 13-inch baking pan.

Baked Meatballs with Pesto and Ricotta

BREAKFAST THROUGH DINNER · SERVES 4 TO 5

½ cup plain fine breadcrumbs

½ cup milk

1 egg

¾ cup finely grated Parmigiano-Reggiano cheese

4 tablespoons finely chopped flat-leaf parsley, divided

3 tablespoons finely chopped basil, divided

3 teaspoons finely chopped oregano, divided

1 shallot

1 garlic clove, finely minced

1½ teaspoons kosher salt

¼ teaspoon black pepper

10½ oz lean ground beef

7 oz mild Italian sausages

Olive oil

1 (28 oz) can crushed tomatoes

½ cup ricotta cheese

½ cup prepared basil pesto

Note:

If you'd like to make your own pesto for these meatballs, whip up a batch from the recipe for Grilled Summer Squash Pizza (page 78).

Aaron's first birthday that we celebrated together fell on the same day he was playing a show at the Rivoli in downtown Toronto. I surprised him with a homemade cake—but no dinner. The next year, when I asked him what he'd like, he answered, "Spaghetti and meatballs." Year after year, his birthday meal has remained the same and, while I'm not sure what recipe I used over a decade ago, these new super-tender meatballs are now his favorite birthday feast.

Preheat your oven to 400°F.

In a small bowl, stir together the breadcrumbs and milk and set aside. In a large bowl, beat the egg and then stir in the Parmigiano-Reggiano along with 3 tablespoons of the parsley, 2 tablespoons of the basil, and 1 teaspoon of the oregano. Grate the shallot into the bowl on the large side of a box grater and add the garlic. Season with the salt and pepper, add the breadcrumb mixture, and stir well to combine.

Add the ground beef to the bowl and split open the sausage casings with the tip of a sharp knife. Squeeze the meat from the casings into the bowl, and discard the casings. Using your fingers almost like rakes, gently and thoroughly mix everything together, being careful not to squeeze the mixture in your hands, as that will lead to tough meatballs.

Divide the mixture into 12 evenly sized pieces and gently roll into large balls. Place the meatballs on a large baking sheet and drizzle with oil to coat. Bake just until browned on the bottom but not yet fully cooked, 10 to 15 minutes. Remove from the oven and set aside. Leave the oven switched on.

In a 9-inch square or round baking dish, combine the tomatoes with 1 tablespoon of oil as well as the remaining 1 tablespoon each of parsley and basil and remaining 1 teaspoon of oregano. Season with salt and pepper and mix to combine. Nestle the meatballs into the tomato sauce and dollop the ricotta over top.

Return the meatballs to the oven until their internal temperature reaches 160°F to 165°F, 20 to 25 minutes. Remove from the oven and spoon the pesto over top before serving as-is or with crusty bread or your favorite pasta.

Aaron's Veggie Chili, Mary's Pot Pie

BREAKFAST THROUGH DINNER · SERVES 6 TO 8

FOR THE CHILI

1 small butternut squash, peeled, seeded, and cut into ½-inch cubes

3 tablespoons olive oil, divided

Kosher salt and black pepper

2 small yellow onions, diced

1 yellow bell pepper, seeded and cut into 1-inch pieces

1 jalapeño pepper, minced

4 garlic cloves, minced

1 (5½ oz) can tomato paste

2 teaspoons Dijon mustard

1½ tablespoons chili powder

2 teaspoons ground cumin

1½ teaspoons smoked paprika

½ teaspoon cayenne pepper

¼ teaspoon ground cinnamon

1 (28 oz) can diced tomatoes

1 (19 oz) can black beans, drained and rinsed

1 (19 oz) can red kidney beans, drained and rinsed

1 (12 oz) package extra firm tofu, cut into 1-inch cubes

1–1½ cups low-sodium vegetable broth

FOR THE TOPPING

1 cup coarse ground yellow cornmeal

½ cup all-purpose flour

½ cup whole wheat flour

¼ cup packed dark brown sugar

2 teaspoons baking powder

1 teaspoon kosher salt

1 cup buttermilk

⅓ cup butter, melted

1 egg

Aaron has a few things in the kitchen that he absolutely crushes. Washing dishes is definitely number one on the list followed closely by his prodigious chili-making skills. This recipe uses his basic formula for the perfect hearty veggie chili with a bit of my own spin on the final product. Topped with slightly sweet whole wheat cornbread, this is a great oven-to-table meal for any day of the week.

Preheat your oven to 400°F.

For the chili, toss the squash with 1 tablespoon of the oil on a baking sheet and season with salt and pepper. Roast until golden brown and tender, 20 to 25 minutes. Set aside.

Meanwhile, place a Dutch oven or large ovenproof saucepan over medium heat and add the remaining 2 tablespoons of oil. Add the onions and bell peppers and season with salt and pepper. Cook, stirring occasionally, until the vegetables are golden brown, 4 to 5 minutes. Add the jalapeños and garlic and continue to cook for another minute, just to cook off the raw garlic flavor.

Stir in the tomato paste, Dijon, chili powder, cumin, paprika, cayenne pepper, and cinnamon, and cook, stirring constantly, for 1 minute to toast the spices, or until the mixture is fragrant. Add the canned tomatoes with their juice, black and red kidney beans, tofu, roasted squash, and enough broth to reach a thick stewy consistency. Season to taste with salt and pepper, then bring to a simmer, uncovered, for 15 minutes.

While the chili simmers, prepare the cornbread topping by whisking together in a mixing bowl the cornmeal, both flours, sugar, baking powder, and salt. Make a well in the center and pour in the buttermilk, melted butter, and egg. Stir just until combined.

Dollop the cornbread mixture over top of the chili and carefully spread it into an even layer so that it reaches the sides of the pot. Bake until the cornbread topping is crisp on top and a skewer inserted into it comes out clean, 20 to 25 minutes.

Serve with sour cream, cheddar, avocado, green onions, and cilantro.

FOR SERVING

Sour cream, grated cheddar
cheese, diced avocado, thinly
sliced green onions, and
finely chopped cilantro

Note:

The untopped chili can be made
up to 2 days in advance and
refrigerated, or up to 2 months
in advance and frozen.

Slightly Updated Mom's Mac and Cheese

BREAKFAST THROUGH DINNER · SERVES 4

Kosher salt

1½ cups dry macaroni

3 eggs

1½ cups milk

½ teaspoon dry mustard powder

Black pepper

2½ cups grated cheddar cheese, divided

20–25 butter crackers, such as Ritz

¼ cup ground Parmigiano-Reggiano cheese (see page 85)

6 tablespoons butter, melted

Custardy and sliceable as opposed to stringy and spoonable, this Southern-style mac and cheese casserole is comfort food at its finest. It's what my mom would make whenever my brother or I needed a pick-me-up, and it was the thing she'd freeze and send with us every autumn as we moved back to university. A big plate of this with a squidge of ketchup on the side is what I crave when I'm in the mood for something homey and ultra-nostalgic.

Preheat your oven to 400°F and grease an 8- or 9-inch round casserole dish or square baking pan with cooking spray.

Set a pot of water to boil over high heat, season well with salt, and cook the macaroni just until al dente. Drain and allow to cool slightly. Meanwhile, whisk the eggs, milk, and mustard powder together in a bowl. Season with ½ teaspoon of salt and a pinch of pepper.

When the pasta has cooled slightly, transfer it to the prepared baking pan. Scatter 1½ cups of the cheddar over top and give it all a gentle mix to distribute the cheese. Pour the egg mixture over the macaroni and set aside while you prepare the topping.

Place the crackers in a bowl or a large resealable plastic bag and crush them up a bit. Add the Parmigiano-Reggiano and melted butter and mix well. Finally, add the remaining 1 cup of grated cheddar and mix to combine. Scatter this topping over the macaroni and bake until set in the middle and golden brown on top, 30 to 35 minutes. Allow the mac and cheese to sit for 10 to 15 minutes to cool slightly before serving.

Pumpkin Gnudi with Blue Cheese

BREAKFAST THROUGH DINNER · SERVES 4

1 cup ricotta cheese

¾ cup canned pumpkin purée (not pumpkin pie filling)

1 garlic clove, finely minced

2 egg yolks

2 teaspoons finely chopped sage

¾ cup finely grated Parmigiano-Reggiano cheese

¼ teaspoon freshly grated nutmeg

½–¾ cup all-purpose flour

1 teaspoon kosher salt

½ teaspoon black pepper

½ cup table (18%) or whipping (35%) cream

4 oz mild blue cheese, such as Gorgonzola or Danish Blue, divided

2 tablespoons extra virgin olive oil

¼ cup finely chopped walnuts

Sage leaves

Gnudi are kind of like if the inside of cheese tortellini had a baby with gnocchi. They are essentially little dumpling pillows of ricotta and Parmigiano-Reggiano cheese, with these ones getting an extra flavor bump from one of my favorite pantry staples, canned pumpkin. It may look fancy, but these pumpkin gnudi with a creamy blue cheese sauce are an absolute cinch to put together.

Combine the ricotta, pumpkin, garlic, egg yolks, and sage in a medium bowl. Stir in the Parmigiano-Reggiano and nutmeg along with ½ cup of the flour, salt, and pepper. Mix just until combined. You should be able to roll a small amount of the mixture into a ball without it sticking to your hands too much. If it does stick, add another ¼ cup of flour and mix just to combine.

Heavily dust a baking sheet with an even layer of flour and, using a standard tablespoon or 1 oz cookie scoop, scoop out the gnudi. Roll them into balls, place on the baking sheet, and press down gently to flatten slightly. Continue until all of the dough is used up. Set aside.

In a small saucepan or skillet, bring the cream to a simmer over medium-low heat and allow it to cook down for 5 minutes, stirring frequently. Crumble in about half of the blue cheese and stir until the sauce is smooth. Season with salt and pepper and turn the heat to low to keep warm.

Bring a large pot of salted water to a boil, add the gnudi, and cook in batches of about 10 pieces for 4 to 5 minutes. You want them to cook for about 1 minute after they float to the surface. Using a slotted spoon, transfer the gnudi to a clean baking sheet and toss with the oil. For crisp gnudi, warm the oil over medium heat in a large nonstick skillet and fry the boiled gnudi until golden, about 2 minutes per side.

Crumble half of the remaining cheese into the warm sauce and stir to combine. Divide the sauce between four serving dishes and top with the gnudi. Serve sprinkled with the chopped walnuts, remaining cheese, and a few sage leaves.

Curried Shrimp Orzo

BREAKFAST THROUGH DINNER · SERVES 4 TO 6

5 cups low-sodium vegetable, shellfish, or chicken broth

3 tablespoons butter

2 small shallots, finely diced

1 celery stalk, finely diced

Kosher salt and black pepper

2 garlic cloves, finely minced

1 tablespoon curry powder

½ teaspoon ground turmeric

1¾ cups dry orzo

½ cup dry white wine, such as Pinot Grigio

1 lb (31–35 count) raw shrimp, deveined and shells removed

½ lemon, zested and juiced

2 tablespoons finely chopped flat-leaf parsley or cilantro

When Aaron and I were in Florence for our honeymoon, we visited a little restaurant near the Mercato Centrale. After placing an order for a bottle of Chianti, we quickly ordered way too many dishes for two people to eat. The trip was a number of years ago now, and there was quite a bit of wine involved, but one of my most vivid memories of that meal was a bowl of the most delicious golden curry goodness. In this recipe, the warming spices of curry powder bring a decidedly cool-weather flavor to this broth-fed, risotto-style orzo.

In a small saucepan, warm the broth over low heat just until hot.

Place a large sauté pan or saucepan over medium-low heat and melt the butter. Add the shallots and celery, season with salt and pepper, and cook, stirring frequently, until a little translucent, about 1 to 2 minutes. Add the garlic, curry powder, and turmeric and cook for 30 seconds to 1 minute, just to cook off the raw garlic and toast the spices. Turn the heat up to medium, add the orzo, and cook for 1 to 2 minutes, stirring frequently, to lightly toast the pasta.

Stirring continuously, add the wine and cook until it has all been absorbed. Using a ladle, add about ½ cup of the hot broth to the orzo and stir to combine. Stir the pasta frequently until all of the broth is absorbed, then add another ½ cup of broth. Continue adding broth in this manner until the orzo is cooked to al dente. This should take about 20 minutes and use anywhere from 4¼ to 5 cups of broth.

When the orzo is just cooked, stir in the shrimp, cover the pan with a lid, and allow the shrimp to cook until pink and opaque, about 3 to 4 minutes. To finish the dish, stir in the lemon zest and juice, season with more salt and pepper, if desired, and sprinkle with the parsley.

Seeded Soda Bread Scones

SNACKS, SIDES, SWEETS, AND SIPS · MAKES 10 SCONES

1 cup whole wheat flour

1 cup all-purpose flour

4 tablespoons shelled pepitas, divided

3 tablespoons sunflower seeds, divided

3 teaspoons sesame seeds, divided

3 teaspoons flax seeds, divided

1½ teaspoons baking powder

1 teaspoon baking soda

1 teaspoon kosher salt

¾–1 cup buttermilk

¼ cup butter

1 tablespoon honey

I was initially going to call this recipe Rock Cakes, but thought that it might call to mind the cooking abilities of Rubeus Hagrid. In order to assuage any worries of broken teeth, know that these tender no-knead rolls are like a mix between Irish soda bread and savory scones and are the perfect thing for tearing up and dunking in soup or stews.

Preheat your oven to 425°F and line a large baking sheet with parchment paper.

In a large bowl, whisk together both flours, 3 tablespoons of the pepitas, 2 tablespoons of the sunflower seeds, 2 teaspoons of the sesame seeds, and 2 teaspoons of the flax seeds. Add the baking powder, baking soda, and salt, and stir well to combine. Set aside.

Place ¾ cup of buttermilk in the freezer to chill for 5 minutes while you melt the butter and honey together in a small saucepan over low heat or in the microwave.

Make a well in the center of the dry ingredients and pour in the chilled buttermilk followed by the melted butter and honey. Using a wooden spoon or rubber spatula, stir until combined, adding up to ¼ cup more buttermilk if the dough looks too dry or floury. Once the dough is too stiff to stir with the spoon, lightly flour a work surface and turn the dough out onto it. Knead the dough once or twice to bring it together, then roll it into an 8- to 10-inch log. Cut the dough into 10 equal pieces and place them, cut-side down, on the prepared baking sheet.

Brush the tops with a little buttermilk and evenly sprinkle over the remaining 1 tablespoon pepitas, 1 tablespoon sunflower seeds, 1 teaspoon sesame seeds, and 1 teaspoon flax seeds. Bake for 12 to 14 minutes until golden brown. Cool the scones on a wire rack, then serve with butter. Store leftover scones in a sealed container at room temperature for up to 2 days.

Fennel Potato Leek Soup

SNACKS, SIDES, SWEETS, AND SIPS · SERVES 4 TO 5

2 tablespoons butter

2 large leeks, white and light green parts only, thinly sliced

1 bulb fennel, cored and thinly sliced, fronds reserved

Kosher salt

12 oz yellow flesh potatoes, peeled and diced small

3½ cups vegetable broth

2 cups milk

½ lemon, juiced

Black pepper

Sour cream, for serving

As the weather starts to chill, soup is to my stovetop what a sweater is to my closet. They are the things I reach for when I'm in the mood for something cozy and comforting, as they somehow seem to have the power to make everything feel just a little bit better.

Place a large saucepan over medium heat and melt the butter.

Meanwhile, place the sliced leeks in a large bowl and cover with tap water. Run your hands through the leeks, agitating them so that any dirt and debris fall away to the bottom of the bowl. Using your hands, scoop the leeks out of the water, allowing as much water as possible to drain away, and add them to the pot along with the fennel. Season with salt and cook for 10 minutes, stirring occasionally. Turn the heat down to medium-low and continue to cook, stirring occasionally, until the leeks and fennel are very tender, about 20 minutes.

Add the potatoes to the pot along with the broth, turn the heat up to medium-high, and bring everything to a boil. Cover and simmer until the potatoes are very tender, 15 to 20 minutes. Remove the soup from the heat and, using an immersion or stand blender, blend until smooth. Return the soup to low heat and stir in the milk.

Just before serving, stir in the lemon juice and season with pepper and a bit more salt. Serve hot, topped with a dollop of sour cream and a few of the reserved fennel fronds.

Auntie Linda's Pumpkin Soup

SNACKS, SIDES, SWEETS, AND SIPS · SERVES 4 TO 6

1 (3–3½ lb) sugar pumpkin or kabocha squash

2 tablespoons butter

1 yellow onion, finely diced

Kosher salt and black pepper

3 garlic cloves, minced

¼ teaspoon ground cinnamon

⅛ teaspoon freshly grated nutmeg

⅛ teaspoon ground cloves

⅛ teaspoon smoked paprika

⅛ teaspoon ground cumin

3–4 cups low-sodium vegetable broth

½ cup whipping (35%) cream, plus more for serving

1 tablespoon pure maple syrup

3–4 tablespoons pepitas, for garnish

When I was growing up, every Thanksgiving was spent at my Auntie Linda's house out in the country. We would visit the farm where she boarded her horse, go on long walks along empty country roads, and sit down to a table groaning under the weight of all of her delicious hard work. It was tradition to start the meal with steaming bowls of the most luxurious and flavorful pumpkin soup I've ever tasted. Auntie Linda passed away a few years back, but every Thanksgiving, I make my spin on the soup and it's like she's right there with us.

Preheat your oven to 375°F.

Place the whole pumpkin in a baking pan. Using a small paring knife, pierce the skin of the pumpkin five or six times, then roast until the flesh is tender and a knife can be easily poked into the center, about 1 hour. Remove from the oven and allow to cool enough to handle.

Once the pumpkin is cool, melt the butter in a medium saucepan over medium heat. Add the onions, season with salt and pepper, and cook, stirring frequently, until the onions are slightly translucent and just beginning to turn golden, about 2 to 3 minutes. Add the garlic, cook for 30 seconds, then stir in the cinnamon, nutmeg, cloves, paprika, and cumin. Allow this to cook for another 30 seconds, then stir in 3 cups of the broth and turn the heat down to low.

Cut the cooled pumpkin in half and scoop out the seeds and discard. Scrape the tender flesh from the skin, place it in the saucepan, and remove the saucepan from the heat. Using an immersion or stand blender, blend the soup until smooth, adding more broth if it's too thick. Return the soup to low heat, and stir in the cream and maple syrup.

When the soup is hot, taste and season with more salt and pepper if needed. Serve with a little more cream swirled through each bowl in true Auntie Linda fashion and garnish with a few pepitas.

Retro Beans

FOR THE BEANS

Kosher salt

¾ lb green beans, trimmed

¾ lb wax beans, trimmed

2 tablespoons butter, divided

8 oz cremini mushrooms, quartered

Black pepper

2 garlic cloves

1½ tablespoons all-purpose flour

½ cup low-sodium vegetable broth

1 cup milk

¼ cup finely grated Parmigiano-Reggiano cheese

FOR THE CRISPY SHALLOTS AND LEEKS

1 leek, thinly sliced and separated, white and light green parts only

Canola oil, for frying

½ cup cornstarch

1 shallot, thinly sliced and separated

Kosher salt

Mid-century Americana at its finest, green bean casserole is a staple on millions of Thanksgiving tables every year. While in Canada we celebrate Thanksgiving over a month before our friends to the south, this retro dish still fits in perfectly with the classic menu of turkey and mashed potatoes. With all of the main ingredients readily available at farmers' markets during the autumn months, I like to make this casserole with a mix of green and wax beans, a homemade mushroom cream sauce, and an updated not-from-a-can topping with homemade crispy shallots and leeks.

Preheat the oven to 400°F and lightly grease an 8- or 9-inch round or square baking dish with cooking spray. Place a large pot of salted water to boil over high heat.

Blanch both beans in the salted water until bright and crisp, 2 to 3 minutes. Remove them from the water and transfer to a bowl of ice water to stop the cooking process.

Melt 1 tablespoon of the butter in a large sauté pan or skillet over medium-high heat and cook the mushrooms until golden brown, about 4 to 5 minutes. Season with black pepper. Turn the heat down to medium-low, add the remaining butter, and stir in the garlic. Cook for 30 seconds, then sprinkle the flour over top. Stir in the flour and allow it to cook for 1 to 2 minutes, just to remove any raw flavor.

Slowly whisk in the broth, followed by the milk, and bring the mixture to a simmer to thicken. Once it has thickened, stir in the Parmigiano-Reggiano and then the blanched beans. Transfer this mixture to the prepared baking dish and set aside.

Before you make the crispy shallots and leeks, place the leeks in a large bowl and cover with tap water. Run your hands through the leeks, agitating them so that any dirt and debris fall away to the bottom of the bowl. Using your hands, scoop the leeks out of the water, allowing as much water as possible to drain away, then transfer to a clean kitchen towel and dry very well.

Heat ½ inch of the oil in a large sauté pan over medium heat. Line a baking sheet with paper towel and set aside. Place the cornstarch in a small bowl, add the shallot slices, and toss to coat. Remove the shallots from the cornstarch, place in a fine mesh sieve and shake to dust off as much excess as possible. Place the shallot slices in the oil to fry until lightly golden brown and crisp, about 2 to 3 minutes. Using a slotted spoon, transfer the fried shallots to the prepared baking sheet and season immediately with salt.

Dredge and fry the leeks in the same way you did the shallots, removing them from the oil when light golden brown and crisp, about 1 to 2 minutes.

Sprinkle the crispy shallots and leeks over the beans and transfer the baking dish to the oven. Bake until bubbling, 15 to 20 minutes, then allow to cool slightly for 5 minutes before serving.

Crispy Brussels Sprouts with Tahini Caesar

1 lb Brussels sprouts, trimmed and halved

3 tablespoons olive oil, divided

Kosher salt and black pepper

¼ cup tahini

1 lemon, zested and juiced

2 garlic cloves, very finely minced

1 tablespoon Dijon mustard

1½ teaspoons red wine vinegar

2 tablespoons extra virgin olive oil

¼ cup capers

¼ cup smoked or salted almonds, roughly chopped

¼ cup finely grated Parmigiano-Reggiano cheese

Everyone and their brother knows what a Brussels sprout looks like. They're tiny little cabbages that, if cooked by my mother in 1998, taste like an old shoe. But on their stalks, Brussels are one of the most fantastical Dr. Seuss-ian vegetables you'll ever behold and, when cooked properly to crispy golden brown in a hot oven, their flavor is a revelation. Caesar salad purists may sneer, but the nutty and slightly bitter tahini plays off the sweetness of the crispy roasted Brussels sprouts and makes a perfect cold weather version of this classic salad.

Preheat your oven to 400°F.

Toss the Brussels sprouts with 2 tablespoons of the oil on a large baking sheet. Season with salt and pepper and roast until golden and crisp, 20 to 25 minutes, stirring about halfway through.

Meanwhile, whisk together the tahini, lemon zest and juice, garlic, Dijon, and vinegar. Add 2 tablespoons of water, the extra virgin olive oil, ½ teaspoon pepper, and salt to taste. Whisk until well combined and set aside.

Heat the remaining 1 tablespoon of oil in a small skillet set over medium-high heat. Drain the capers well and dry them off on paper towel. Add the capers to the skillet and fry until crisp, about 1 minute, being careful of splatter. Using a slotted spoon, transfer the capers to paper towel to drain.

When the Brussels sprouts are roasted, spread the Caesar dressing over a serving dish and top with the sprouts. Scatter the capers, almonds, Parmigiano-Reggiano, and a little more pepper, if desired, over top.

Note:

This makes a great vegan side dish if you omit the grated Parmigiano-Reggiano.

Roasted Cauliflower and Radicchio with Anchovies and Brown Butter

SNACKS, SIDES, SWEETS, AND SIPS · SERVES 4 TO 6

1 cauliflower, cut through the core into 8 wedges

3 tablespoons olive oil, divided

Kosher salt and black pepper

1 medium head radicchio, cut through the core into 4 wedges

¼ cup butter

2 tablespoons whipping (35%) cream

4–6 anchovy fillets, finely minced

2 garlic cloves, minced

1 lemon, zested and juiced

½ teaspoon crushed red pepper flakes

2 tablespoons finely chopped flat-leaf parsley

2 teaspoons finely chopped sage

Roasting cauliflower is like culinary magic. The high heat of the oven brings out the loveliest sweet caramelized flavor, which pairs so well with the subtle, bitter-sweetness of roasted radicchio. Dressed with nutty brown butter and briny, funky anchovies, this is the perfect side to any autumn meal.

Preheat your oven to 400°F.

Place the cauliflower wedges on a large baking sheet. Drizzle with 2 tablespoons of the oil, season with salt and pepper, and toss to coat. Lay the cauliflower cut-side down and roast for 25 minutes or until the underside is golden.

Meanwhile, toss the radicchio wedges with the remaining 1 tablespoon of oil and season with salt and pepper. When the underside of the cauliflower is golden, give it a toss, add the radicchio to the pan, and continue to roast until the cauliflower is tender and golden brown and the radicchio is wilted and slightly charred, 10 to 15 minutes.

In a small saucepan or skillet, warm the butter and cream together over medium heat to melt the butter. Cook until the mixture is lightly browned, stirring occasionally, about 2 minutes. Add the anchovies and cook for another 1 to 2 minutes to marry the flavors. Remove the pan from the heat and stir in the garlic, lemon zest and juice, and red pepper flakes.

When the cauliflower and radicchio are done, transfer them to a plate, spoon over the browned anchovy and lemon butter, and scatter the parsley and sage on top.

Bourbon Brown Butter Rice Krispie Squares

½ cup butter

1 (10 oz) bag miniature marshmallows, divided

2 tablespoons bourbon

1 teaspoon vanilla extract

5¾ cups Rice Krispies or other crispy rice cereal

1 tablespoon chocolate sprinkles, such as Callebaut's Mini Crispearls (optional)

The only way to improve the already perfect sweet treat that is a Rice Krispie square is by adding brown butter and a splash of bourbon to the mix. Smoky, slightly nutty, and oh-so-gooey, these slightly grown-up squares would round out a brown-bag lunch quite nicely, if you ask me.

Grease a 9-inch square baking pan with cooking spray or line the bottom and sides with parchment paper.

Place a large saucepan over medium heat and add the butter. Cook the butter, stirring frequently with a wooden spoon or heatproof spatula, until lightly browned, about 2 to 3 minutes.

Turn the heat down to low and add 4 cups of the marshmallows, stirring frequently until almost melted. Stir in the bourbon and vanilla and continue to cook until fully melted and smooth. Remove the pan from the heat and stir in the rice cereal and remaining marshmallows until well combined.

Using a rubber spatula greased with a little cooking spray, scrape the mixture into the prepared baking pan and press it down into an even layer. Immediately scatter the top with the chocolate sprinkles (if using) and set aside to cool completely to room temperature before cutting into 16 equal squares. Store any leftovers in a resealable container for up to 1 week.

Note:
A good cue that your butter is browned is the bubble size and sound. The butter will become bubbly rather than foamy and it will sound quiet, with a little sizzle.

That Classic Sandwich Cookie

SNACKS, SIDES, SWEETS, AND SIPS · MAKES 20 SANDWICH COOKIES

FOR THE COOKIES

1¼ cups butter, room temperature

¾ cup packed light brown sugar

½ cup sugar

1 egg white

1 teaspoon vanilla extract

2 cups all-purpose flour

1 cup black cocoa powder

1 teaspoon kosher salt

½ teaspoon baking soda

FOR THE FILLING

¼ cup butter

¼ cup vegetable shortening

½ teaspoon vanilla extract

1¾ cups icing sugar

½ teaspoon kosher salt

Note:

This dough can be frozen for up to 3 months, so you can have freshly baked cookies whenever the craving strikes. Simply slice, bake, and fill as directed.

Black cocoa powder is what gives these cookies that classic sandwich cookie look and flavor. It can be found at specialty food shops or certain bulk food stores. If you can't find it, feel free to use Dutch process cocoa powder. The resulting cookies will be more akin to a fudgy version of the classic, which, if you ask me, isn't a bad thing at all.

For the cookies, in a mixing bowl, or a stand mixer fitted with a paddle attachment, cream together the butter and both sugars on high speed until light and fluffy, about 2 minutes, scraping down the bowl once or twice. Beat in the egg white and vanilla, scrape down the bowl, and set aside.

In a separate bowl, sift together the flour, cocoa powder, salt, and baking powder. Add the dry ingredients into the creamed butter mixture and mix on low speed just until combined. Divide the dough in half and lay each piece on a sheet of plastic wrap. Form each piece of dough into a 2-inch-diameter cylinder, wrap snugly in the plastic, and refrigerate for 4 hours, or up to overnight.

When you're ready to bake, preheat your oven to 350°F and line two large baking sheets with parchment paper. Retrieve the logs of dough from the fridge and, using a sharp knife, slice them into ¼-inch-thick disks. Place the cookies on the prepared baking sheets, being sure to leave at least 1 inch between each one, and bake until matte and cooked in the center, 8 to 11 minutes. Cool the cookies completely on the baking sheets.

Meanwhile, make the filling by beating together the butter, shortening, and vanilla on high speed until well combined. Add the icing sugar ¼ cup at a time, mixing well after each addition and scraping down the sides of the bowl. When all of the icing sugar has been incorporated, add the salt and beat the filling on high speed for 30 seconds to give it a fluffy texture.

Spread or pipe the filling on to half of the cooled cookies and top with the remaining cookies.

These are best if enjoyed within 2 days but will keep in a tightly sealed container at room temperature for 1 week.

Pumpkin Pecan Pudding

SNACKS, SIDES, SWEETS, AND SIPS · SERVES 4

¾ cup pure pumpkin purée (not pumpkin pie filling)

1 egg

½ cup milk

½ teaspoon vanilla extract

⅔ cup packed dark brown sugar

½ teaspoon ground cinnamon

½ teaspoon ground ginger

¼ teaspoon freshly grated nutmeg

⅛ teaspoon ground cloves

¼ teaspoon kosher salt

⅔ cup pecan halves

When it comes to cooler-weather desserts, I feel like there are two types of people: pumpkin people and pecan people. Whether you're like my family and firmly on Team Pumpkin (pie, if we're getting specific) or you side with the nuts, this custardy baked pumpkin pecan pudding will please every palate.

Preheat your oven to 350°F and set a kettle of water to boil. Place four (¾-cup) ramekins in a 9-inch square baking pan and set aside.

In a large bowl, whisk together the pumpkin purée, egg, milk, and vanilla. Add the sugar, cinnamon, ginger, nutmeg, cloves, and salt and whisk well to combine. Carefully pour this pumpkin mixture into the ramekins and arrange the pecans over top.

Carefully pour 1 inch of boiling water around the ramekins in the baking pan. Transfer the pan to the oven and bake until the pumpkin mixture is set but still slightly jiggly in the center, 35 to 40 minutes. Remove the ramekins from the water and enjoy warm, or let cool completely, cover, and refrigerate overnight. These puddings will keep tightly covered in the fridge for up to 3 days.

No-Bake Coffee and Cream Cheesecake

SNACKS, SIDES, SWEETS, AND SIPS · MAKES 1 (9-INCH) CHEESECAKE

9 oz chocolate-dipped digestive biscuits

5 tablespoons butter, melted

⅛ teaspoon kosher salt

1½ cups whipping (35%) cream

2 cups brick-style cream cheese, cut into pats

¾ cup sugar

1 tablespoon instant espresso powder

2 teaspoons vanilla extract

¼ cup finely chopped chocolate-covered espresso beans

Note:

Plain digestive biscuits will also work if you can't find the chocolate-dipped variety.

In my house, autumn ushers in the start of dinner party season. It might be the change in the weather or the slow lengthening of dusk, but this is when invites start to go out to my friends and family to come over and enjoy a cozy dinner at my place. I always want to have a dessert to serve but I don't always want to heat my house on those few balmy autumn days. This simple no-bake cheesecake combines the classic combo of coffee and cream without my ever having to turn on the oven or coffee maker.

Prepare a 9-inch springform pan by spraying the bottom and sides with cooking spray and lining the sides with a collar of parchment paper.

Place the digestive biscuits in a food processor fitted with a steel blade and pulse until finely ground. Pour in the melted butter, season with the salt, and pulse to combine. Transfer this mixture to the prepared springform pan and, using your hands or the bottom of a glass, tamp it down to form a bottom crust. Refrigerate it while you make the filling.

In a mixing bowl, or a stand mixer fitted with a whisk attachment, whip the cream on high speed until stiff peaks form, about 2 minutes. Transfer to a separate bowl and set aside. If using a stand mixer, replace the whisk attachment with a paddle attachment, and beat the cream cheese and sugar together on high speed until light and fluffy, about 2 minutes.

Using a rubber spatula, fold the whipped cream into the cream cheese mixture in two additions. In a small bowl, stir the espresso powder in the vanilla until fully dissolved. Gently stir the mixture into the cheesecake filling until it is almost fully combined but with a few streaks remaining.

Retrieve the crust from the fridge and pour the cheesecake filling on top, shimmying the pan to smooth the surface. Scatter the outside rim of the cheesecake with the espresso beans and refrigerate, uncovered, until firm, about 6 hours.

To serve, unlatch the springform pan and peel away the parchment collar from the sides of the cheesecake. Slice with a clean warm knife for perfect pieces. This cheesecake will keep covered in the fridge for up 5 days.

Peanut Butter and Banana Cream Pie

SNACKS, SIDES, SWEETS, AND SIPS · MAKES 1 MILE-HIGH PIE

FOR THE CRUST

14 oz (about 30 cookies) filled peanut butter cookies, such as Nutter Butters or Pirate cookies

¼ cup butter, melted

FOR THE FILLING

1 tablespoon gelatin powder

3 cups milk, divided

½ cup sugar, divided

½ teaspoon kosher salt

½ vanilla bean, scraped, or 2 teaspoons vanilla extract

¼ cup cornstarch

4 egg yolks

4 tablespoons butter

¾ cup smooth sweet peanut butter (see note)

3 bananas, thinly sliced

FOR THE TOPPING AND ASSEMBLY

½ cup brick-style cream cheese, room temperature

1½ cups whipping (35%) cream

3 tablespoons icing sugar

¼ vanilla bean, scraped, or 1 teaspoon vanilla extract

¼ teaspoon butter extract or butterscotch extract (optional)

Banana chips (optional)

Chocolate shavings (optional)

I really love close-up magic. So when Aaron and I found ourselves in Los Angeles for work, I made it my mission to scrounge up an invite to the Magic Castle, the clubhouse for the Academy of Magical Arts. We had drinks, requested songs from Irma the piano-playing ghost, enjoyed a ton of close-up magic, including the classics of turning kerchiefs into doves and pulling rabbits from hats, and had an entertainingly retro dinner starting with shrimp cocktail and ending with the best darn banana cream pie I've ever had. Here's my take on that perfect dish. And for my next trick, turn the page and get ready to be hungry!

Preheat your oven to 375°F and lightly grease a 9-inch springform pan with cooking spray. Place the pan on a large baking sheet and set aside.

For the crust, in a food processor fitted with a steel blade, pulse the cookies until very finely ground. Add the melted butter and pulse to combine. Turn the crumb mixture out into the prepared springform pan and, using your hands or the bottom of a glass, tamp it into the bottom and up the sides of the pan so that it makes a 2½- to 3-inch-high crust. Bake until very lightly golden, 10 to 12 minutes. Set aside to cool completely.

Meanwhile, prepare the filling by sprinkling the gelatin over ¼ cup of cold water, stirring to ensure that it is well combined. Set aside to allow the gelatin to bloom.

In a medium saucepan, combine 2½ cups of the milk with ¼ cup of the sugar, salt, and vanilla bean pulp and pod (if using), and set it over medium heat. Bring this mixture to a simmer and stir frequently to dissolve the sugar.

In a medium bowl, whisk the remaining ¼ cup of sugar with the cornstarch and add the egg yolks and remaining ½ cup of milk. While continually whisking, slowly stream the hot milk mixture into the egg mixture. This tempering helps ensure that you do not scramble the egg yolks with the hot milk. Pour the tempered egg and milk mixture back into the pot and, while constantly stirring with a whisk, bring the mixture to a low boil and cook until the mixture thickens and coats the back of a spoon or reaches 165°F on an instant-read thermometer. When thickened, whisk in the bloomed gelatin and stir until fully dissolved and combined.

Remove the pot from the heat and whisk in the butter, peanut butter, and vanilla extract (if using). Pass the filling through a fine mesh sieve into a large bowl to remove any lumps. Scatter the sliced bananas over the bottom of the prepared crust. Pour the filling over the bananas into the prepared crust, press a piece of plastic wrap directly over the surface of the filling, and place the pie in the fridge for at least 4 hours but preferably overnight to set.

When the filling has set, prepare the topping for the pie by beating the cream cheese on high speed in a mixing bowl, or a stand mixer fitted with a whisk attachment, until smooth. Add the whipping cream, icing sugar, and vanilla bean pulp or extract, as well as the butter extract or butter-scotch extract (if using) and whip to stiff peaks, about 2 to 3 minutes.

Dollop or pipe on the whipped cream topping and scatter the pie with banana chips and/or chocolate shavings (if using).

Serve immediately or store the pie in the fridge lightly covered for up to 4 days.

Note:
Natural or freshly ground varieties of peanut butter will make the filling a little greasy and too liquid-y, so be sure to use a classic smooth peanut butter like Kraft or Skippy.

Concord Grape Mulled Cider

1½ lb Concord grapes, stems removed, plus extra for garnish

4 cups apple cider

¼ cup pure maple syrup

10 whole cloves

10 green cardamom pods

6 allspice berries

3 whole star anise

3 cinnamon sticks

½ teaspoon black peppercorns

6 oz apple brandy (optional)

Thinly sliced apple

The unsung hero of autumn fruits, Concord grapes taste exactly how you think grapes should taste. Tart, juicy, and definitely grapey, these dark indigo bunches put every grape-flavored food item to shame. For the few short weeks when they take over market stalls and grace the shelves of my supermarket, my fingers are stained purple from overindulgence. Take a back seat, apples, because Concord grapes are here to shine.

In a large saucepan, combine the grapes and cider with 2 cups of water, the maple syrup, cloves, cardamom, allspice, star anise, cinnamon, and peppercorns and place over medium heat. Bring the mixture to a boil, then turn the heat down to medium-low. Allow the cider to simmer for 20 minutes, stirring and mashing the grapes against the side of the pot occasionally, then remove it from the heat and allow the flavors to meld and steep for 10 to 15 minutes.

To serve, add 1 oz of apple brandy (if using) to each mug and pour the hot mulled cider through a fine mesh sieve over top to strain out any of the mulling spices or grape skins. Garnish with a thin slice of apple and a small cluster of Concord grapes.

Keep any remaining cider warm over low heat until ready to serve.

Peach Cardamom Rye Smash

SNACKS, SIDES, SWEETS, AND SIPS · MAKES 1 COCKTAIL

½ peach, roughly chopped

1½ oz rye

1 oz Peach Cardamom Simple Syrup (see below)

1 oz peach or orange juice

1 dash Angostura or orange bitters

Ice cubes

Splash soda water

Dried apricot or peach slice, for garnish

Here in Ontario, peach season runs from late summer into early autumn. Wanting to harness the last few weeks these farm-fresh fruits are still available, I gave this cocktail a decidedly autumnal spin with the warming spice of cardamom and the pepperiness of rye.

In a cocktail shaker, combine the roughly chopped peach with the rye, simple syrup, peach juice, and bitters. Using a wooden spoon or a cocktail muddler, mix everything together while smashing up the peach. Add about ½ cup of ice to the shaker, seal it up, and shake vigorously for 20 seconds to chill.

Place a few ice cubes in a rocks glass and strain the chilled cocktail over top. Add a splash of soda water and serve immediately, garnished with a dried apricot or peach slice.

Peach Cardamom Simple Syrup

MAKES ENOUGH SYRUP FOR 5 COCKTAILS

1 peach, roughly chopped

½ cup sugar

1 tablespoon green cardamom pods, lightly crushed

In a small saucepan set over medium-low heat, combine the peach, sugar, and cardamom pods with ½ cup of water. Bring to a simmer and cook, stirring occasionally, until the sugar has fully dissolved, about 2 minutes.

Cover the pot, remove it from the heat, and allow the syrup to steep for 15 minutes. Strain the syrup into a resealable container and refrigerate for up to 2 weeks.

Cinnamon Boulevardier

Ice cubes

2 oz bourbon

1 oz Campari

1 oz sweet vermouth

2 dashes orange bitters

Ground cinnamon

Orange peel

1 cinnamon stick

My friend Kyle has a canned response to any activity worth doing and any food worth eating: "Best paired with a Negroni." My husband, Aaron, tends to agree, but sometimes he craves something a little richer and more caramel-y. So, I've brought in the Negroni's woodsy cousin, the Boulevardier, which is essentially a combination of his two favorite cocktails: a Negroni and a Manhattan.

Fill a cocktail shaker or a large glass halfway with ice and add the bourbon, Campari, sweet vermouth, orange bitters, and a pinch of ground cinnamon. Stir well for 10 to 15 seconds, then strain into a rocks glass containing 1 or 2 ice cubes.

Using a lighter or a match, lightly burn the orange peel and cinnamon stick. Rub the orange peelalong the rim of the glass, then add it into the drink along with the cinnamon stick.

Winter

Rich, Satisfying, and Celebratory

Crispy French Toast with Maple Orange Butter

BREAKFAST THROUGH DINNER · SERVES 4

6 eggs

½ cup milk

¼ cup maple syrup, plus more for serving

½ teaspoon vanilla extract

1 orange, zested

½ teaspoon ground cinnamon

⅛ teaspoon kosher salt

2 cups crispy rice cereal, such as Rice Krispies

8 thick slices challah

2 tablespoons butter, divided

Canola oil, for frying

Maple Orange Butter, for serving (see page 191)

If there is one box of breakfast cereal I always have in my house, it's Rice Krispies. Their trio of mascots seem to be the only ones who haven't fallen victim to a "cool" redesign, which I very much appreciate. The cereal is essential for one of my favorite sweet treats (see page 170), and it is the only ingredient I can think of that adds that specific crispy crunch to any recipe. Paired with the most delicious maple orange butter, this classic staple gives French toast a bit of a zhuzh and makes for a two-for-one breakfast that's perfect for a cold winter morning.

Preheat your oven to 200°F and place a baking sheet on the middle rack.

In a large shallow dish or baking pan, whisk the eggs, milk, maple syrup, vanilla, orange zest, cinnamon, and salt together and set aside. Scatter the cereal into a smaller shallow dish and set aside.

Heat a large skillet over medium heat and place 2 slices of bread in the egg mixture, allowing them to soak for 20 to 30 seconds per side. Once soaked, press the bread into the cereal, flipping once so that each side is well coated. When you're ready to fry, melt ½ tablespoon of the butter with a little splash of oil in the pan and cook 2 slices of the cereal-coated bread until golden brown on each side, 3 to 4 minutes per side.

Place the French toast on the baking sheet in the oven to keep warm and continue preparing and cooking the remaining slices of bread.

Serve with Maple Orange Butter and maple syrup.

Maple Orange Butter

MAKES ABOUT ¼ CUP

¼ cup butter

2 teaspoons maple syrup

½ orange, zested

1 teaspoon brown sugar

¼ teaspoon kosher salt

In a small bowl, mix together the butter, maple syrup, orange zest, sugar, and salt until well combined. Use immediately or cover and refrigerate for up to 1 month.

Holiday Breakfast Sandwich

BREAKFAST THROUGH DINNER · MAKES 8 BREAKFAST SANDWICHES

8 Everything Bagel Drop Biscuits (page 194)

1 cup spreadable or room-temperature brick-style cream cheese, cut into pats

1 garlic clove, very finely minced

2 tablespoons very finely chopped chives or green onions

1 tablespoon very finely chopped flat-leaf parsley

¼ cucumber, thinly sliced

Dill (optional)

12–14 oz cold-smoked salmon

2½–3 tablespoons drained capers

Black pepper

For as long as I can remember, our Christmas morning breakfast has always been a straightforward and delicious spread of bagels, smoked salmon, and cream cheese. It might have been my mom's way of staying sane during the busy holidays, but that relatively simple breakfast has remained our tradition even now that Aaron and I host Christmas morning at our house. Instead of going the fully store-bought route, though, I opt to make a platter of these. Homemade everything bagel biscuits are topped with the easiest and most scrumptious herb and garlic cream cheese, layers of cold-smoked salmon, and a good helping of dill, pepper, and my mom's favorite, salty little capers.

Preheat your oven to 250°F, place the biscuits on a baking sheet, and reheat them in the low oven for 15 to 20 minutes. If you have just made the biscuits fresh, you can skip this step as they should still be warm from the oven.

Place the cream cheese, garlic, chives, and parsley in a small bowl and mix together until well combined.

To assemble the sandwiches, slice each biscuit in half like you would a burger bun. Spread the bottom half with a couple of tablespoons of the cream cheese mixture and top with a few slices of cucumber, dill (if using), and smoked salmon. Top with the capers and some pepper. Cover with the biscuit tops and serve immediately.

Everything Bagel Drop Biscuits

BREAKFAST THROUGH DINNER · MAKES 8 BISCUITS

1¾ cups all-purpose flour

2 teaspoons baking powder

½ teaspoon kosher salt

¼ teaspoon garlic powder

½ cup butter, cold, cut into pats

½ cup brick-style cream cheese, cold, cut into pats

2 green onions, thinly sliced

1 cup buttermilk, well shaken, cold, plus more for brushing

Everything Bagel Topping, see below

Everything Bagel Topping

MAKES ABOUT ⅓ CUP

2 tablespoons sesame seeds

2 tablespoons poppy seeds

4 teaspoons dried minced onion

2 teaspoons dried minced garlic

1½ teaspoons kosher salt

In a small resealable container, mix together the sesame seeds, poppy seeds, dried minced onion, dried minced garlic, and salt. Cover and store in a dark, dry place for up to 6 months.

What's the difference between a normal biscuit and a drop biscuit, you ask? Well, it's really all in the shaping. Classic layered biscuits involve the slightly messy process of folding the dough over itself in order to make the layers, while drop biscuits go straight from the mixing bowl onto the baking pan and into the oven. These biscuits are as good for breakfast as they are served in a basket on your dinner table, and they're about a thousand times easier to make than homemade bagels.

Preheat your oven to 425°F and line a large baking sheet with parchment paper.

Stir together the flour, baking powder, salt, and garlic powder in a large bowl. Cut in the butter using two butter knives or by snapping and rubbing the butter and the flour mixture with your fingers. Add the cream cheese and continue to cut or snap the mixture together until the cream cheese and butter are about the size of large peas. Stir in the onions, then the buttermilk just until combined, adding a splash more if the mixture won't hold together.

Using a 2 oz ice cream scoop or two large spoons, scoop 8 biscuits onto your prepared baking sheet. Brush the tops with buttermilk, then scatter a good pinch of Everything Bagel Topping on each biscuit. Bake the biscuits until cooked through and golden brown, 20 to 25 minutes. Transfer to a wire rack and allow to cool slightly before eating.

To store, cool completely to room temperature and store in the fridge in a resealable container for up to 4 days. Reheat in a low oven, the microwave, or a toaster to freshen them up.

French Onion Soup Buns with Prosciutto

BREAKFAST THROUGH DINNER · MAKES 12 BUNS

FOR THE DOUGH

3½–4 cups bread flour

1 tablespoon sugar

2¼ teaspoons instant dry yeast

1½ teaspoons kosher salt

½ cup milk

¼ cup butter, melted

1 large egg

FOR THE FILLING

3 tablespoons butter

3 yellow onions, halved and thinly sliced

½ teaspoon kosher salt

Black pepper

1½ teaspoons herbes de Provence

2 tablespoons brandy

2 tablespoons Dijon mustard

7 oz Gruyère cheese, grated and divided

8–10 slices prosciutto, about 3½ oz

1 egg yolk

1 tablespoon milk

The nooks and crannies of a swirled bun shouldn't be reserved only for a mixture of cinnamon and sugar. Layers of swirls are a great way to bring the cheesy, salty flavors of old favorites like French onion soup to your breakfast table or as a satisfying anytime snack.

For the dough, in a large bowl, or a stand mixer fitted with a dough hook, combine 3½ cups of bread flour with the sugar, yeast, and salt.

Heat the milk and butter over low heat or in the microwave just until the butter melts. Let the mixture sit until it is just above body temperature, then add it along with ¾ cup of very warm tap water to the flour mixture. Stir until a shaggy dough forms, then knead the dough on medium-low speed for 5 to 6 minutes, adding more flour as needed, 1 tablespoon at a time, until the dough forms a ball and is springy when touched.

Transfer the dough to a large lightly greased bowl, cover with plastic wrap or a dinner plate, and allow it to rise in a warm place until doubled in size, 1 to 1½ hours.

Meanwhile, prepare the filling by melting the butter in a large frying pan over medium heat. Add the onions to the pan along with the salt, some pepper, and the herbes de Provence. Turn the heat down to medium-low, and cook, stirring occasionally, until the onions are golden and caramelized, about 20 to 25 minutes. Deglaze the pan with the brandy and stir well for 1 to 2 minutes while the liquid cooks away. Remove from the heat and allow the onions to cool to room temperature.

When the dough has risen, grease a 9- × 13-inch baking pan with cooking spray and line the bottom with parchment paper. Punch down the dough and turn it out onto a lightly floured surface. Roll the dough into a 14- × 22-inch rectangle. Evenly spread the Dijon over the dough, followed by the caramelized onions. Scatter three-quarters of the cheese over the onions, then lay on the prosciutto in an even layer. With a long edge of the rectangle facing you, roll the dough into a log and pinch the seam to seal.

Using a sharp knife, cut the log into 12 equal pieces. Arrange in the prepared baking pan, loosely cover with plastic wrap and a clean kitchen towel, and place the buns back in a warm spot to rise for 45 to 60 minutes until almost doubled in size.

Preheat the oven to 375°F.

Beat the egg yolk and the 1 tablespoon of milk together to make an egg wash and lightly brush it over the tops of the buns. Scatter with the remaining cheese and bake for 40 to 45 minutes until golden brown and springy to the touch and the internal temperature of the buns has reached 185°F to 190°F. Allow the buns to cool slightly in the pan before digging in. Tightly cover and store leftover buns in the fridge for up to 3 days, reheating before enjoying.

Note:
When filling these buns, I like to leave half without prosciutto for those who, like me, are non-ham-eating hams.

Banh Mi Beef Dip

BREAKFAST THROUGH DINNER · SERVES 4

FOR THE BEEF

2 lb beef blade or chuck roast

½ teaspoon kosher salt

½ teaspoon black pepper

½ teaspoon ground allspice

½ teaspoon ground ginger

2 teaspoons vegetable oil

2 teaspoons sesame oil

2 cups low-sodium beef broth

¼ cup soy sauce

¼ cup hoisin sauce

4 whole star anise

2 (each 3 inches) cinnamon sticks

1 stalk lemongrass

1 (3-inch) piece fresh ginger

3 garlic cloves

10–15 cilantro stems, leaves removed and reserved

FOR THE BEET AND CARROT QUICK PICKLES

½ cup white vinegar

2 tablespoons sugar

1½ tablespoons kosher salt

1 large carrot, peeled

1 medium beet, peeled

FOR THE SANDWICHES

1 baguette

¼ cup mayonnaise

3 tablespoons hoisin sauce

½ cucumber, thinly sliced

½–1 Thai bird's eye chili, thinly sliced

1 green onion, thinly sliced

Cilantro leaves, reserved from stems

Sriracha

I'm not going to beat around the bush here. Like any beef dip, this sandwich does take a bit of planning and time but, even though it may look like a long and involved recipe, it really isn't. After a quick sear, the beef hangs out in the oven unattended while you make some simple quick pickles. Then all that's left to do is wait for that beef to be ultra-fork-tender before you assemble one of the prettiest beef dips I've ever seen.

Set the beef on a baking sheet and, using paper towel, pat dry the roast. In a small bowl, mix together the salt, pepper, allspice, and ginger. Rub this mixture all over the roast and allow it to come up to room temperature, about 20 to 30 minutes.

Preheat your oven to 325°F and set a large Dutch oven over medium-high heat.

Add both oils to the pot, followed by the roast. Sear the roast until very well browned all over, about 5 minutes per side. Return the roast to the baking sheet.

Carefully add the broth, soy sauce, hoisin sauce, star anise, and cinnamon in the Dutch oven and bring to a boil. Meanwhile, cut the lemongrass into three or four pieces, slice the ginger into ¼-inch disks, and smash the garlic cloves. Add these aromatics, along with the seared roast and any collected juices, to the Dutch oven, cover, and cook in the oven until fork-tender, 4½ to 5 hours.

Meanwhile, make the beet and carrot quick pickles by bringing the vinegar, sugar, salt, and ½ cup of water to a simmer in a medium saucepan over medium heat to dissolve the sugar and salt. Remove from the heat and set aside.

Cut the carrot and beet into 2- to 3-inch-long matchsticks and place them in separate bowls or small jars. Cover each with the warm pickling liquid and refrigerate for at least 3 hours, or up to 1 month.

Remove the beef from the cooking liquid, place in a large bowl, and use two forks to shred it. Strain the cooking liquid through a fine mesh sieve and keep warm in a small pot set over low heat for serving.

To assemble the sandwiches, cut the baguette into four equal pieces. Slice almost all the way through the side of the baguette, spread the mayonnaise and hoisin sauce on the bottom of each sandwich, and layer on the cucumber and pulled beef. Top each sandwich with beet and carrot quick pickles, a scattering of sliced chilies and green onions, some cilantro, and a squeeze of sriracha.

Serve each sandwich with a small dish of the warm cooking liquid for one heck of a fun beef dip.

Lemon Ginger Orzo Soup

BREAKFAST THROUGH DINNER · SERVES 6

1 medium sweet potato, peeled and cut into 1-inch pieces

2 tablespoons olive oil, divided

Kosher salt and black pepper

½ yellow onion, thinly sliced

2 celery stalks, thinly sliced

2 garlic cloves, finely minced

3–4 tablespoons finely grated fresh ginger

1 tablespoon ground turmeric

6 cups chicken or vegetable broth

1 cup dry orzo

1 lb medium-firm tofu, cut into 1-inch pieces

2 cups roughly chopped Tuscan kale or curly green kale

3 tablespoons finely chopped flat-leaf parsley

1 lemon, juiced

Thinly sliced red finger chili (optional)

Whenever Aaron or I feel a winter cold coming on, you'll find a big pot of this soup bubbling away on our stove. I first developed this recipe as a homemade healthier version of that neon yellow noodle soup that comes in a sachet, and, if you ask me, a cold-busting noodle soup just isn't all it could be without the addition of a ton of ginger and turmeric.

Preheat your oven to 425°F.

Place the sweet potatoes on a baking sheet, toss with 1 tablespoon of the oil, and season with salt and pepper. Roast until slightly golden and cooked through, 20 to 25 minutes. Set aside.

Heat the remaining 1 tablespoon of oil in a large pot over medium heat. Add the onions and celery, season with salt and pepper, and cook, stirring frequently, just until they begin to soften, about 1 to 2 minutes. Add the garlic, ginger, and turmeric and continue to cook for an additional minute.

Add the broth to the pot, turn the heat up to high, and bring to a boil. Once boiling, stir in the orzo and cook until the orzo is about halfway cooked, 5 to 6 minutes. When the pasta has reached a toothy consistency, add the tofu, kale, and roasted sweet potatoes. Continue to boil the mixture until the orzo is fully cooked, the tofu and sweet potatoes are warmed through, and the kale is nicely wilted, 3 to 4 minutes.

Just before serving, stir in the parsley and lemon juice and season with salt and pepper. Serve the soup topped with a scattering of finely sliced chilies, if using.

Jalapeño Mac and Cheese

BREAKFAST THROUGH DINNER · SERVES 4

FOR THE PASTA

Kosher salt

8 oz dry shell pasta

2 tablespoons butter

1 shallot, finely diced

2 jalapeño peppers, seeded and finely diced, divided

Black pepper

1 garlic clove, finely minced

3 tablespoons all-purpose flour

2 cups milk, warmed

1 teaspoon Dijon mustard

½ cup herb and garlic cream cheese

1 cup grated Pepper Jack or jalapeño Havarti cheese

1 cup grated extra-old white cheddar cheese

½ cup grated Parmigiano-Reggiano cheese

¼ cup pickled jalapeños, finely chopped

FOR THE TOPPING

1 egg

3 tablespoons milk

2 thick slices white country bread, roughly torn into nickel-sized pieces

½ cup grated Pepper Jack or jalapeño Havarti cheese

¼ teaspoon kosher salt

It might sound like an odd addition to a Christmas feast, but jalapeño mac and cheese has been a staple at our family celebrations ever since my cousin Crystal introduced us to it a few years back. The spice of the jalapeño is mellowed in the cooking process but still provides enough of a zing to cut through the creamy sauce. This mac and cheese is great baked and served on your holiday dinner table or as a big bowl of cheesy stovetop mac without the topping for a casual weeknight meal.

Preheat your oven to 425°F. Grease an 8- or 9-inch square baking dish with cooking spray and set aside.

Set a large pot of well-salted water to a boil over high heat. When the water has come to a rolling boil, add the pasta and cook just until al dente. Drain the pasta and set aside.

Meanwhile, in a large pot, melt the butter over medium-low heat. Add the shallots and half of the jalapeños, season with salt and pepper, and cook, stirring frequently, until the shallots are translucent and just starting to turn golden brown, 3 to 4 minutes. Add the garlic, evenly sprinkle the flour over top, and turn the heat up to medium. Cook for 2 to 3 minutes, whisking frequently, to cook off the raw garlic flavor and toast the flour.

Very slowly start to add the warmed milk, about ¼ cup at a time, whisking constantly in order to avoid lumps. After the first couple of additions, the mixture will most likely look a little clumpy but just keep whisking and slowly adding milk. The lumps will cook out. When all of the milk is added, stir in the Dijon and bring the mixture to a simmer for 4 to 5 minutes, just to thicken.

Whisk in the cream cheese and slowly begin to add the Jack, cheddar, and Parmigiano-Reggiano. Whisk until the cheeses are fully melted and the sauce is thick and creamy.

Turn the heat down to low and, switching to a large spoon or heatproof spatula, fold in the remaining fresh jalapeños along with the pickled jalapeños and cooked pasta. Season with more salt and pepper.

Transfer the mac and cheese to your prepared baking dish and set aside.

In a small bowl, make the topping by whisking the egg and milk together. Add the bread, cheese, and salt and stir until well combined. Spread this mixture over the mac and cheese and bake until golden and bubbling, 20 to 25 minutes.

Tomato and Kale Baked White Beans

BREAKFAST THROUGH DINNER · SERVES 4

3 tablespoons butter

1 yellow onion, finely diced

Kosher salt and black pepper

1 pint cherry or grape tomatoes

2 garlic cloves, finely minced

1 (28 oz) can whole tomatoes

1 (19 oz) can white kidney beans

1 small Parmigiano-Reggiano rind (optional)

4 cups roughly chopped Tuscan or curly green kale

1 tablespoon finely chopped flat-leaf parsley

2 teaspoons finely chopped oregano

½–1 teaspoon crushed red pepper flakes

Coarsely grated Parmigiano-Reggiano, extra virgin olive oil, and crusty bread, for serving

I cannot tell you how many times during the depths of winter I've been hoodwinked into buying the world's saddest, mealiest large tomato. As a tomato optimist, I try to convince myself that, even in cold climates, large imported tomatoes can still provide that summer-fresh flavor, but I'm always wrong. In any case, I think I've finally learned my lesson. When it comes to using big tomatoes in winter, the best option is to go with a can.

Preheat your oven to 375°F.

In a large saucepan or ovenproof skillet, melt the butter over medium heat, add the onions, and season with salt and pepper. Cook the onion until translucent and just starting to turn golden brown around the edges, about 2 to 3 minutes. Add the cherry tomatoes and cook until they begin to burst, about 5 minutes. Stir in the garlic and the canned tomatoes and, using a wooden spoon, break up canned tomatoes so that they release some of their juices. Allow this to come to a simmer.

Meanwhile, drain and rinse the kidney beans. When the tomato mixture is simmering, add the beans, Parmigiano-Reggiano rind (if using), kale, parsley, oregano, and red pepper flakes. Season with more salt.

If you're using an ovenproof skillet, cover it with the lid or aluminum foil and place it in the oven for 20 minutes. If you're using a saucepan, transfer the mixture to a 9-inch square baking dish, cover with aluminum foil, and place in the oven for 20 minutes. After 20 minutes remove the foil and continue to bake until the top is just starting to color and look a little crisp, 10 to 15 minutes.

Remove the beans from the oven and immediately top with Parmigiano-Reggiano, a pinch of salt, and a drizzle of oil. Serve with crusty bread and extra cheese.

Note:
Canned whole tomatoes like to make a bit of a mess when you burst them, so be careful and avoid wearing white.

Beef Bourguignon

8 oz thick-cut bacon, diced

2 lb chuck beef, cut into 1-inch cubes

Kosher salt and black pepper

5 tablespoons all-purpose flour, divided

4 tablespoons butter, divided

2 yellow onions, peeled and cut into 8 to 10 wedges

3 large carrots, cut diagonally into 1-inch chunks

3 garlic cloves, minced and divided

½ cup brandy

1 (750 ml) bottle dry red wine, such as Pinot Noir or Côtes du Rhône

2 cups low-sodium beef broth

1 tablespoon tomato paste

2 large sprigs thyme

10–15 flat-leaf parsley stems

2 bay leaves

1 teaspoon brown sugar

10–12 oz mushrooms, quartered

2 shallots, finely diced

¼ teaspoon freshly grated nutmeg

2–3 teaspoons balsamic vinegar

2–3 tablespoons finely chopped flat-leaf parsley

In my years of recipe writing, I've come to realize that not everyone has a collection of half a dozen Dutch and French ovens that their husband struggles to find storage for. If, unlike me, you do not collect insanely heavy cookware, there are a few work-arounds when it comes to making something like beef bourguignon that goes from the stove to the oven. The first option is to do all of the stovetop work in a large pot and transfer the stew to an ovenproof dish with a tight-fitting lid. Another option is to simply use a metal-only pot on the stove and cover it tightly with aluminum foil when it goes into the oven. No matter your kitchen equipment, beef bourguignon is winter comfort at its best and should go on the menu as soon as the cold weather blows in.

Preheat your oven to 300°F.

Place the bacon in a large Dutch or French oven or ovenproof pot and place over medium heat. Allow the bacon to render some of its fat and cook just until crisp. Transfer to a plate and set aside.

Meanwhile, place the beef in a mixing bowl and season well with salt and pepper. Sprinkle 2 tablespoons of the flour over top and give it a good toss to evenly coat. Turn the heat up to medium-high and add 1 tablespoon of the butter to the hot bacon fat along with one layer of the flour-coated beef. You do not want the beef to overlap, as that will cause some of it to steam rather than sear. Allow the beef to sear on all sides, about 2 to 3 minutes per side, then remove it from the pan and continue to sear in batches until all of the beef is well browned.

Remove the last of the beef from the pan, add the onions and carrots, and cook, stirring frequently, for 2 to 3 minutes. Add about half of the garlic, then carefully add the brandy to deglaze the pan. If you are using a gas range or simply want to show off, you can flambé here, but to avoid unscheduled flare-ups, I suggest turning the heat off before adding the brandy and turning it on again once it's in the pan. Using a wooden spoon, scrape the bottom of the pan to release all of the cooked-on bits, then add the wine, broth, tomato paste, and seared beef along with any juices that have collected, and bring the mixture to a boil.

CONTINUES

Using some butcher's twine, make a little bundle out of the thyme sprigs and parsley stems. This makes them easier to remove later. Add this bundle along with the bay leaves and sugar to the pot, cover, and cook in the oven for 1 hour.

After 1 hour, transfer the pot from the oven to the stove, turn the heat on to medium, remove the lid, fish out the thyme and parsley bundle, and allow the stew to simmer until the liquid is reduced by one-third and the beef is very tender, 25 to 30 minutes.

While the stew simmers away, place a large pan over medium heat and melt 1 tablespoon of the butter. Add the mushrooms and shallots, season with salt and pepper, and cook, stirring frequently, just until golden, about 5 to 6 minutes. Add the remaining garlic and the nutmeg, cook for an additional minute, and then transfer the mushroom mixture to the same plate as the cooked bacon.

In the same pan over medium heat, make a roux by melting the remaining 2 tablespoons of butter and whisking in the remaining 3 tablespoons of flour. Cook, whisking frequently, until the mixture is pale gold in color, about 2 to 3 minutes.

When the roux is done, ladle about ½ cup of the stew liquid into the roux and whisk to combine. Whisk in another 1 cup of the liquid and transfer the whole mixture into the pot with the stew. Add the bacon and mushrooms and stir to mix. Allow the stew to keep simmering for 10 minutes to thicken up.

Just before serving, add the balsamic and parsley and season with more salt and pepper.

80s Chicken

BREAKFAST THROUGH DINNER · SERVES 4

4 boneless, skin-on chicken breasts (see note)

Kosher salt and black pepper

½ cup all-purpose flour

1 tablespoon olive oil, divided

1 tablespoon butter, divided

1 shallot, finely diced

2 garlic cloves, finely minced

¾ cup table (18%) or whipping (35%) cream

½ cup low-sodium chicken broth

1½ teaspoons Dijon mustard

½ cup finely grated Parmigiano-Reggiano cheese

½ lemon, juiced

⅓–½ cup oil-packed julienned sundried tomatoes

3–4 cups roughly chopped Tuscan or curly green kale

Note:

If you prefer chicken thighs (or just happen to get a good deal on them at the grocery store), feel free to swap 8 chicken thighs for the breasts. Bone-in definitely works, but my crowd prefers boneless as they are much easier to eat.

I have a note in my phone that I wrote on a bleary-eyed, slightly tipsy red-eye flight from Toronto to Paris that reads: "Sundried tomatoes, spinach, and cream sauce? 1988 called and wants its food back but GUESS WHAT? YOU CAN'T HAVE IT BECAUSE IT'S A DELICIOUS COMBO AND I WANT IT." I don't know what inspired that rant, but the note inspired this dish. Sure, the kale should probably be spinach if I'm really going to stick to what a sleep-deprived Mary was talking about, but I'm channeling her laissez-faire attitude and doing what I want.

Preheat your oven to 400°F and place a large sauté pan or cast iron skillet over medium-high heat.

Set out your chicken on a clean work surface and pat it dry with paper towel. Season well with salt and pepper. Scatter the flour into a shallow dish and add the chicken, tossing to coat each breast.

When your pan is hot, add half of the oil and butter and allow the butter to melt. Place the chicken in the pan, skin-side down, and sear until golden brown, about 8 minutes. Flip the chicken over, cook for 2 minutes, then transfer to a baking sheet, and place in the oven to continue cooking until the internal temperature reaches 165°F, 8 to 10 minutes. Remove the chicken from the oven and allow it to rest while you make a pan sauce.

Turn the heat under the pan to medium and add the remaining oil and butter. Add the shallots, season with salt and pepper, and cook just until translucent, 1 to 2 minutes. Add the garlic, cook for another 30 seconds, and then carefully pour in the cream and broth.

Allow the sauce to simmer until slightly thickened, about 5 minutes, then whisk in the Dijon, Parmigiano-Reggiano, lemon juice, sundried tomatoes, and kale. Season with salt and pepper, then add the chicken to the pan, lower the heat to medium-low, and simmer for 5 minutes to bring everything together.

A Golden Bird

1 (12–14 lb) turkey, fresh or frozen and fully thawed

¼ cup butter, room temperature

Kosher salt and black pepper

1 small handful flat-leaf parsley sprigs

1 bunch sage

1 bunch thyme

1 yellow onion, quartered

1 head garlic, halved crosswise

1 clementine, unpeeled, halved

¾ cup mayonnaise

4 cups low-sodium chicken broth

It is Christmas 1993. My mom has the family feast all ready to go in the oven and suddenly my brother and dad come down with the flu. But having put in most of the effort to plan, shop, and prep, my mom decided to serve dinner anyway. She made Lipton's chicken noodle soup for the two sickies, leaving the turkey, mashed potatoes, and Brussels sprouts for us. The table was beautifully set. My mom placed the turkey down lovingly. The boys could barely keep from turning green, they were so sick. And my response? "I don't like that big chicken."

Line a roasting pan with a wire rack, and place the turkey, breast side up, on the rack. Remove the giblets from the neck or cavity, to use as a base for gravy if you'd like, and let the turkey come up to room temperature, about 30 minutes. Dry the inside and outside of the bird with paper towel. Meanwhile, preheat the oven to 350°F.

In a small bowl, season the butter with ½ teaspoon of salt and a pinch of pepper. Pinch 2 tablespoons' worth of parsley leaves off the sprigs, pick about 12 sage leaves from the bunch, and strip 5 thyme sprigs of their leaves. Finely chop the herbs, set half aside, and add the remaining half to the butter. Stir until well combined. Gently separate the skin from the breast of the turkey and, using a spoon or your hands, spread the butter under the skin, pushing and spreading it as far and evenly as possible. Season the turkey liberally with salt and pepper and stuff the cavity with the remaining unchopped parsley, sage, and thyme as well as the onions, garlic, and clementine halves.

In a separate bowl, stir together the mayonnaise and remaining chopped herbs and spread a thin layer evenly over the skin of the turkey, discarding any remaining mayo. Tie the legs of the bird together, tuck the wings underneath, and pour the broth into the bottom of the pan, but not over the bird.

Roast the turkey until the internal temperature of the thickest part of thigh reaches 165°F, about 3 to 3½ hours. If the broth evaporates and the bottom of the pan becomes dry, add more broth or water. If the turkey is browning too quickly, tent it with foil.

When the turkey is fully cooked, remove it from the oven, cover it with a loose tent of aluminum foil, and allow it to rest for 30 to 40 minutes before carving.

Note:
Mayonnaise might sound like a strange ingredient to use on a turkey but I find it is easier to spread over the bird and creates a more even golden-brown color than butter. I got the idea originally from my brother, who introduced me to a grilled cheese made with mayo rather than butter.

Prawn Cocktail

SNACKS, SIDES, SWEETS, AND SIPS · SERVES 4

FOR THE SHRIMP

4 cups ice cubes

3 tablespoons kosher salt

2 tablespoons sugar

2 teaspoons celery salt

1 lemon, halved

1 lb (21–25 count) raw shrimp, shell-on and deveined

FOR THE SAUCE

½ cup mayonnaise

2 tablespoons ketchup

½ teaspoon lemon zest

1 teaspoon lemon juice

2 teaspoons prepared horseradish

1 teaspoon Worcestershire sauce

Tabasco sauce

Celery salt

Finely chopped chives (optional)

When I was growing up, shrimp rings were a party staple in our house year round, but on very special occasions, mainly Christmas dinner, my mom would go the extra mile and bust out the most retro and perfect presentation. A set of martini glasses that had never once been graced by booze would be dusted off, lined with a lettuce leaf, and filled with arguably too much cocktail sauce for one serving. Half a dozen shrimp would be hung off the rim. This version deviates slightly from her original recipe by using a rich and creamy Marie Rose sauce, but any way you serve it, this is retro fanciness at its finest.

For the shrimp, prepare an ice bath by adding the ice to a large bowl. Top with just enough water to cover the ice and set aside.

In a large pot, combine 4 cups of water with the salt, sugar, and celery salt. Juice the lemon into the water and add the rinds to the pot. Turn the heat to medium-high and bring the mixture to a boil.

Add the shrimp and cook until they are pink and still plump, 1½ to 2 minutes. Using a slotted spoon, transfer the shrimp to the ice bath and allow them to chill for a few minutes while you make the sauce.

For the sauce, whisk together the mayonnaise, ketchup, lemon zest and juice, horseradish, and Worcestershire sauce. Season with Tabasco sauce and celery salt.

Remove the shrimp from the ice bath and dry them off with a clean kitchen towel or paper towel. Serve on a large plate with the sauce in a small serving dish, scattered with finely chopped chives (if using). If you are feeling fancy and want to pull a real Myra Berg here, serve in a martini glass or coupe lined with a lettuce leaf.

Note:
The shrimp can be fully prepared and stored in the fridge up to 1 day in advance. The sauce will keep in a resealable container in the fridge for up to 1 week.

Smoked Salmon Spread

SNACKS, SIDES, SWEETS, AND SIPS · MAKES ABOUT 2½ CUPS

1 cup brick-style cream cheese, room temperature

½ cup soft goat cheese

7 oz cold-smoked salmon

2 radishes, trimmed and finely minced

1½ tablespoons chopped capers

1 tablespoon finely chopped dill

1 tablespoon finely chopped chives

1½ teaspoons finely chopped flat-leaf parsley

½ lemon, zested and juiced

Black pepper

During the winter, my pantry and fridge are always well stocked with ingredients and dishes I can throw together to make a quick snack board. Whether it's made up of a few different types of cheese, some homemade crackers, pickled veg, or premade dips and spreads, snack boards become a lifesaver for those times when people stop in for a quick visit or when a dinner party spills into a sleepover thanks to too much fun, too much wine, or too much snow. This smoked salmon spread is the perfect thing to have on hand for a mid-afternoon drop-in, a pre-dinner snack, or even, along with a few toasted bagels, the breakfast table.

In a mixing bowl, or a stand mixer fitted with a paddle attachment, beat together both cheeses on high speed until smooth.

Cut the smoked salmon into small bite-sized pieces and add it to the cheese mixture along with the radishes, capers, dill, chives, parsley, and lemon zest and juice. Beat on medium speed just until combined.

Season with pepper and serve as an appetizer with crudités, crackers, and sliced baguette or as breakfast or brunch with toasted bagels.

You can store any leftovers in a resealable container in the fridge for up to 5 days.

Mushroom and Lentil Sausage Rolls

SNACKS, SIDES, SWEETS, AND SIPS · MAKES 16 ROLLS

¼ cup chopped walnuts

2 teaspoons olive oil

1 small shallot, finely diced

2 cups roughly chopped mushrooms

Kosher salt and black pepper

1 tablespoon butter

1 garlic clove, finely minced

1½ teaspoons finely chopped sage

1½ teaspoons finely chopped thyme

½ teaspoon fennel seeds

1½ teaspoons brandy

2 teaspoons soy sauce

1 teaspoon balsamic vinegar

¼ cup cooked green lentils (see note)

1½ teaspoons lemon juice

1 sheet frozen puff pastry, thawed

1 egg

2 teaspoons sesame seeds

There are really only two things I miss since I stopped eating beef, poultry, and pork over 15 years ago: buffalo wings and sausage rolls. It's not the meat itself that I miss but rather the whole experience that surrounds these two flavorful bites. There is no pub food more perfect than the spicy and saucy buffalo wing, and I really can't think of a more classic holiday appetizer than flaky sausage rolls. It took a few tries, but these veg-friendly sausage rolls provide all of the savory and buttery crispiness of their meaty cousins without any of the actual meat.

Preheat your oven to 450°F and line a baking sheet with parchment paper.

In a large dry skillet, toast the walnuts over medium heat, stirring frequently, until they begin to smell nutty, about 5 minutes. Transfer them to a food processor fitted with a steel blade and set aside.

To the same pan, add the oil and shallots. Cook over medium heat until the shallots are translucent and just beginning to color, 2 to 3 minutes, then add the mushrooms and season well with salt and pepper. Allow the mushrooms to cook down for 5 to 7 minutes, stirring occasionally, before adding the butter, garlic, sage, thyme, and fennel seeds. Turn the heat up to medium-high and continue to cook for another 2 to 3 minutes, until golden brown.

Deglaze the pan with the brandy, soy sauce, and balsamic and cook, stirring constantly, until all of the liquid has evaporated. Transfer the mushroom mixture to the food processor along with the cooked lentils and lemon juice. Pulse six to eight times to chop everything up and bring the mixture together, being careful not to make a smooth purée. Give the mixture a taste and season with more salt and pepper if desired. Set aside.

Lightly dust a work surface with flour and unroll the sheet of puff pastry. Cut the pastry in half so that you have two long rectangles. In a small bowl, beat the egg well with 2 teaspoons of water to make an egg wash.

Canned lentils (drained and rinsed) work well for this recipe, but if you'd like to cook your own, combine ¼ cup of picked over green lentils with ½ cup of water and bring to a boil over medium-high heat. Cover, turn the heat down to low, simmer until tender, 20 to 30 minutes, then season with kosher salt. This will make about double the amount of lentils you need for this recipe but leftovers can be refrigerated in a resealable container for up to 4 days.

Using damp hands, shape half of the mushroom mixture into a sausage shape the same length as the puff pastry. Place it in the center of one of the pastry rectangles, brush the pastry edges with egg wash, then fold one side of the pastry over, pressing the seam to seal. Repeat this process with the remaining mushroom mixture and pastry.

Cut each log into 8 equal sausage rolls, transfer to the prepared baking sheet, and brush with the remaining egg wash. Scatter the tops with sesame seeds and bake until deep golden brown, 16 to 18 minutes.

Serve with your favorite dips.

Mom's Pecan Brandy Baked Brie

SNACKS, SIDES, SWEETS, AND SIPS · SERVES 8 TO 10

2 sheets frozen puff pastry, thawed

1 (14–16 oz) wheel of Brie

1 egg

1 tablespoon milk

3 tablespoons dark brown sugar

3 tablespoons finely chopped pecans

3 tablespoons finely chopped raisins, California or Thompson

½ teaspoon kosher salt

¼ teaspoon black pepper

1½ tablespoons brandy

Have I given my mom a bit of a bum rap when it comes to her skills in the kitchen? Maybe, but there is a common denominator when it comes to those dishes that she truly excels at, and that is the glorious no-fail combination of starch and cheese.

Preheat your oven to 375°F and line a baking sheet with parchment paper.

Lay 1 sheet of pastry on the baking sheet and place the wheel of Brie in the center. In a small bowl, beat together the egg and milk to make an egg wash. Brush the egg wash on the pastry around the Brie so that it creates about a 1-inch border, but don't brush right to the edges of the pastry. In a small bowl, mix together the sugar, pecans, raisins, salt, pepper, and brandy. Spoon this over top the Brie. Lay the second sheet of pastry over top and press firmly to seal the edges.

Using a sharp knife, trim around the Brie, leaving that 1-inch border, and give the edges one more press and crimp to ensure they are sealed. Brush the top and sides with some more egg wash and bake until deep golden brown, 25 to 30 minutes.

Allow the baked Brie to rest for at least 15 to 20 minutes before arranging on a rimmed serving dish with sliced baguette and crackers.

Note:
Cut the puff pastry scraps into rough shapes and bake along with the Brie for little bonus puff pastry crackers.

Super-Crispy Roast Potatoes

3 lb yellow flesh potatoes, cut into 8 to 10 wedges

4 teaspoons kosher salt, divided

1 teaspoon baking soda

6 tablespoons olive oil, divided

2 tablespoons cornstarch

¼ cup plain fine breadcrumbs

Black pepper

These potatoes are inspired by my brilliant friend Simon, dinner party host and crispy potato maker extraordinaire. Simon also introduced me to the glory and drama of a candlelit dinner party, the thought being that while your guests will see and taste only chic deliciousness, you as the host get to worry less about the dishes waiting in the sink and whether your meal looks perfectly golden brown. By shutting off the lights and scattering candles around the table, everything somehow looks and tastes infinitely more delightful and time seems to slow, making a delicious dinner stretch into the wee hours.

Place the potato wedges in a large pot and cover with cold water. Stir in 3 teaspoons of the salt and the baking soda and bring to a boil, uncovered, over high heat. Allow the potatoes to boil just until barely fork-tender, about 6 to 7 minutes, then drain and allow to air-dry.

Coat the bottom of a large baking sheet with 3 tablespoons of the oil and place it in the bottom third of a cold oven. Turn the oven on and preheat to 450°F.

While the oven heats, transfer the potatoes to a large bowl and toss with the remaining 3 tablespoons of oil. Sprinkle on the cornstarch, breadcrumbs, and remaining 1 teaspoon of salt. Season with pepper and, using a rubber spatula, gently toss the potatoes for 1 to 2 minutes to develop some of the potato starches.

Carefully remove the baking sheet from the oven and place the potatoes on it in a single layer, cut-side down. Roast until the undersides of the potatoes are a deep golden brown, 18 to 22 minutes. Flip the potatoes over and continue to roast until crisp and golden all over, 13 to 15 minutes.

Remove the potatoes from the oven, season immediately with more salt and pepper, and transfer to a serving dish. Serve with whatever condiments you like best. My personal favorite is a good dollop of mayonnaise.

Roasted Fennel and Beet Salad

SNACKS, SIDES, SWEETS, AND SIPS · SERVES 4

8 small beets

2 bulbs fennel

2 tablespoons olive oil, divided

Kosher salt and black pepper

3½ oz feta cheese

½ cup Greek yogurt

½ lemon, zested and juiced

1 garlic clove, very finely minced

1 tablespoon finely chopped dill

2 teaspoons finely chopped tarragon

2 teaspoons finely chopped flat-leaf parsley

1–2 teaspoons prepared horseradish

1–2 anchovies packed in oil, very finely minced

Extra virgin olive oil

Licorice-y fennel and earthy beets become so perfectly sweet and tender after a long roast in the oven. Great served warm or cold, this dish can be prepared up to 3 days in advance, making it one of my favorite quick winter salads. The only thing I would hold off on doing until just before serving is broiling the feta. That way, you get the most wonderful flavor and textural contrast between the creamy feta and the golden-brown broiled bits.

Preheat your oven to 375°F.

Trim the tops and bottoms off the beets and fennel, reserving some of the fennel fronds. Place the beets on a piece of aluminum foil or in an ovenproof dish fitted with a lid. Drizzle with 1 tablespoon of the oil, season with salt and pepper, and tightly cover the beets with another piece of aluminum foil or the lid. Cut the fennel bulbs through the root end into 8 wedges each and place them on a baking sheet. Drizzle with the remaining 1 tablespoon of oil and season with salt and pepper.

Roast the beets and fennel until the fennel is tender and golden brown and a sharp knife can easily pierce the beets, 40 to 50 minutes, flipping the fennel halfway through. It is possible that the fennel might be done before the beets, so keep an eye on both. Beets sometimes take a little longer to cook based on their size, age, and where they've been stored.

Allow the beets and fennel to cool enough to handle. Using a small paring knife, peel and quarter the beets. Set aside.

Turn the oven on to broil and crumble the feta in large chunks into a small baking dish. Place the feta under the broiler until golden brown on top, 3 to 5 minutes.

Meanwhile, make the dressing by combining the yogurt, lemon zest and juice, dill, tarragon, parsley, and the horseradish and anchovies to taste. Season with salt and pepper.

To plate, spread the dressing onto a serving dish and top with the beets, fennel, feta, and some of the reserved fennel fronds. Drizzle with a little extra virgin olive oil and season with a bit more salt and pepper, if desired.

Upright Potato Gratin

SNACKS, SIDES, SWEETS, AND SIPS · SERVES 4 TO 6

1 lb (about 2 to 3 medium) yellow flesh potatoes, peeled

1 lb (about 2 medium) sweet potatoes, peeled

1 small red onion

1¼ cups whipping (35%) cream

¼ cup finely ground Parmigiano-Reggiano cheese (see page 85)

2 teaspoons Dijon mustard

½ teaspoon kosher salt

¼ teaspoon black pepper

2 teaspoons chopped sage

⅛ teaspoon freshly grated nutmeg

4 oz Gruyère cheese, grated

If you've ever had the pleasure of meeting my mom, Myra, you'll know that she is one heck of a lady. Caring, funny, and kind, she is the best mom I could imagine. I could give you stories of her helping me with my homework, caring for me when I've been sick, or cheering me up when I'm glum, but I think my favorite instance of her fierce love and protective nature was when, while serving me a mounding plate of scalloped potatoes, she accidentally dropped some of the delicious scalding mixture onto my wrist and, without missing a beat or even putting down the dish or serving spoon, swooped down and licked it off my flailing arm. Moms. They truly are the best.

Preheat your oven to 350°F and grease an 8-inch round or 1½-quart baking dish with softened butter or cooking spray.

Cut the yellow and sweet potatoes and red onion into very thin rounds. Set the prepared baking dish out on a work surface and begin stacking the rounds in an alternating pattern in the dish. You want them standing on their edges. Continue stacking and placing the potatoes and onion into the dish in a spiral or straight pattern until they are all used.

In a medium bowl or a glass measuring cup, whisk together the cream, Parmigiano-Reggiano, Dijon, salt, pepper, sage, and nutmeg. Pour this over the potatoes and onions and tightly cover the dish with aluminum foil.

Bake for 30 minutes. Remove the foil, sprinkle with the Gruyère, and bake, uncovered, until the potatoes are cooked through and the cheese is golden brown, about 30 more minutes. Allow to cool for 10 minutes before serving.

Braised and Dressed Cabbage

SNACKS, SIDES, SWEETS, AND SIPS · SERVES 4 AS A MEAL OR 8 AS A SIDE

1 small head Savoy cabbage

2 tablespoons butter

2 garlic cloves, thinly sliced

¼–½ teaspoon crushed red pepper flakes

Kosher salt and black pepper

1½ cups low-sodium vegetable or chicken broth

1 egg

¼ cup milk

4 thick slices country bread, white or whole wheat

2 tablespoons finely chopped flat-leaf parsley, divided

2 teaspoons finely chopped sage, divided

1 lemon, zested and juiced

4 oz soft goat cheese

Having avoided all forms of brassica oleracea as a kid, I'm so happy to have finally hopped on the cabbage bandwagon, with it becoming a staple in my vegetable drawer over the past few years. Braised slowly over low heat, the sweetness of Savoy starts to shine, and the savory stuffing-like dressing makes this dish perfect as a side or as a meal served with grilled or roasted sausages.

Place the cabbage on its root end and slice into 12 wedges through the core and root. Set aside.

In a large Dutch oven, melt the butter over medium heat. Add the garlic and red pepper flakes and season with salt and pepper. Cook for about 30 seconds to take the edge off the garlic, then add the cabbage wedges, season with more salt and pepper, and continue cooking, stirring occasionally, just until the cabbage starts to get a little golden brown on the edges, 3 to 4 minutes.

Turn the heat down to medium-low and pour the broth over the cabbage. Cover the pot with a tight-fitting lid or aluminum foil and allow the cabbage to braise until the parts near the core are tender, 18 to 20 minutes.

Meanwhile, in a mixing bowl, whisk together the egg and milk. Tear the bread into small pieces and add it to the bowl, along with 1 tablespoon of the parsley and 1 teaspoon of the sage. Season with salt and pepper and stir well to combine.

When the cabbage is tender, remove the lid, stir in the remaining 1 tablespoon parsley and 1 teaspoon sage, along with the lemon zest and juice, then top with the bread mixture. Dot the goat cheese over top and place the pot on the middle rack of your oven. Set the oven to broil until the top is browned and set, 5 to 6 minutes.

Serve as a side to any meal or as an accompaniment for roasted meat or sausages.

Note:
If you do not have a Dutch oven, use a large pot, then transfer the cooked cabbage to an ovenproof dish to be topped and finished in the oven.

Broccolini à la Renée

SNACKS, SIDES, SWEETS, AND SIPS · SERVES 4

1 (14 oz) bunch broccolini

2 tablespoons olive oil

Kosher salt and black pepper

1 tablespoon lemon juice

1 tablespoon apple cider vinegar

1 garlic clove, very finely minced

1 teaspoon Dijon mustard

1 teaspoon pure maple syrup

¼ teaspoon ground cinnamon, plus more for serving

2 tablespoons extra virgin olive oil

¼ cup roughly chopped almonds

3½–4 oz soft goat cheese

¼ cup dried cranberries

My friend Renée makes a salad that I request she bring every time she comes for dinner. She spends at least 20 minutes washing and cutting up kale into bite-sized pieces, and then adds cranberry goat cheese and toasted almonds. It's a great blend of bitter, salty, and sweet. Here I've changed it up a bit by substituting the kale with roasted broccolini, which brings more of a side rather than salad vibe to the dish. If you don't love the bitterness of broccolini, feel free to substitute baby broccoli or regular broccoli cut into florets.

Preheat your oven to 375°F.

Trim the stems of the broccolini to freshen up the ends, place them on a large baking sheet, and toss with the olive oil and a good pinch of salt and pepper. Roast just until tender and the leaves begin to crisp slightly, 10 to 15 minutes, tossing halfway through.

Meanwhile, make a dressing by whisking together the lemon juice, vinegar, and garlic in a small bowl. Whisk in the Dijon, maple syrup, and cinnamon, then, while continuing to whisk, slowly stream in the extra virgin olive oil. Season with salt and pepper and set aside.

In a small dry skillet set over medium heat, toast the almonds, stirring frequently, until fragrant and just starting to turn golden brown in spots. This should only take 1 to 2 minutes. Remove the almonds from the pan and set aside.

When the broccolini is roasted, transfer it to a serving dish and drizzle the dressing over top. Crumble on the soft goat cheese and top with the dried cranberries and toasted almonds. Season with salt, pepper, and a pinch of ground cinnamon.

Tartiflette

SNACKS, SIDES, SWEETS, AND SIPS · SERVES 4 TO 6

4–5 medium yellow flesh potatoes, peeled or unpeeled

Kosher salt and black pepper

8 oz slab bacon or thick-cut bacon, diced

2 teaspoons butter

2 shallots, thinly sliced

1 garlic clove, minced

½ cup dry white wine

10–12 oz Reblochon, Taleggio, or Camembert cheese, sliced

⅛ teaspoon freshly grated nutmeg, divided

⅓ cup whipping (35%) cream

A few years ago, Aaron and I took a trip to Paris for New Year's with our friends Marisa and Geoff. For a gal who relishes a food-based itinerary no matter the occasion, our bistro-hopping, market-perusing, grocery-store-shopping, home-cooking trip was the most perfect way to celebrate the start of a new year. On our lengthy walks of the city we came across many holiday markets selling mulled wine, raclette, and the amazing potato/bacon/cheese concoction known as tartiflette. Aaron went so bonkers for it that I had to figure out how to make it myself.

Preheat your oven to 400°F and set a large pot of cold water on the stove.

Add the potatoes to the pot, season the water with salt, and cover with a lid. Bring the potatoes to a boil over high heat and cook until tender, 15 to 20 minutes. Drain the potatoes and allow them to cool slightly before slicing about ¼-inch thick.

Meanwhile, place an 8-inch cast iron skillet or ovenproof frying pan on the stove and add the bacon. Turn the heat on to medium and cook until the bacon starts to sizzle. Add the butter and shallots and season with salt and pepper. Cook the bacon and shallots until the shallots are golden brown, 4 to 5 minutes. Add the garlic, cook for 1 minute just to soften, then carefully deglaze the pan with the wine. Allow the wine to bubble away until almost all of the liquid has evaporated, 4 to 5 minutes.

Using a slotted spoon, remove the bacon and shallots from the pan and set aside. Layer in half of the potatoes followed by half of the bacon and shallot mixture. Lay half of the cheese on top, sprinkle on half of the nutmeg, and repeat the layers to use up the remaining ingredients. Carefully pour the cream over the whole lot and transfer the pan to the oven. Bake the tartiflette until everything is bubbling and golden brown, 10 to 15 minutes. Allow the tartiflette to cool slightly for 5 to 10 minutes before serving.

Brown Butter Sour Cream Glazed Doughnuts

SNACKS, SIDES, SWEETS, AND SIPS · MAKES 12 DOUGHNUTS AND 12 DOUGHNUT HOLES

FOR THE DOUGHNUTS

¼ cup + 3 tablespoons butter

2½ cups all-purpose flour

½ cup packed brown sugar

1 tablespoon baking powder

½ teaspoon kosher salt

¼ teaspoon freshly grated nutmeg

1 cup sour cream

¼ cup buttermilk

1 egg

1 teaspoon vanilla extract

Canola oil, for deep-frying

FOR THE GLAZE

1½ cups icing sugar

5–6 tablespoons milk, warmed

3 tablespoons browned butter, reserved from doughnuts

¾ teaspoon vanilla extract

¼ teaspoon kosher salt

⅛ teaspoon freshly grated nutmeg

As a kid, I had no interest in fun doughnuts. Sprinkled extravaganzas and double chocolate dips, get out of here! The only doughnuts for me were an old-fashioned plain, a walnut crunch (which I'm sure goes down in history as the grossest-looking doughnut ever created), and, my all-time fave, the sour cream glazed. I have always loved its gnarly appearance with those weird little nooks and crannies of dough that make for so much extra texture. The only way they could be better? Brown butter, obviously.

For the doughnuts, in a small saucepan, melt the butter over medium heat, stirring frequently. It will start to sputter and a frothy foam will develop on the top. During this stage, the butter popping will sound loud, then it will mellow out a bit and sound more like a sizzle and the foam on top will become more bubbly than foamy. At this stage, your butter should be nicely browned, containing little golden-brown milk solids. The key to getting perfectly browned butter is not leaving it alone and always keeping an eye on it, as it can go from browned to burnt in a flash. When the butter is browned, immediately remove it from the heat, transfer to a small bowl, and set aside.

In a large bowl, whisk together the flour, sugar, baking powder, salt, and nutmeg and stir well to combine. In a separate bowl, whisk together the sour cream, buttermilk, egg, vanilla, and ¼ cup of the browned butter. Make a well in the center of the dry ingredients and add the sour cream mixture. Stir just until a soft dough forms.

Cover the bowl with plastic wrap or a dinner plate and refrigerate for 1 hour.

Meanwhile, prepare the glaze by whisking the icing sugar, 5 tablespoons of the warm milk, reserved 3 tablespoons of browned butter, the vanilla, salt, and nutmeg together in a small bowl. The glaze should just coat the back of a spoon. If it is a little thick, add another tablespoon of warmed milk. Cover the glaze's surface directly with plastic wrap and set aside at room temperature.

CONTINUES

Remove the dough from the fridge and heat about 2 inches of oil in a large Dutch oven over medium heat. A thermometer should register 355°F to 365°F. If you do not have a thermometer, heat the oil until it shimmers or the end of a wooden spoon causes bubbles to form when gently dipped into it.

Prepare a draining station for your doughnuts by lining a baking sheet with paper towel and a wire rack.

On a generously floured work surface, roll out your chilled dough to ½-inch thickness and, using a 3-inch round cutter, cut out as many rounds as possible. Using a 1-inch round cutter, remove the center of each circle, giving you doughnuts and doughnut holes. Gather the remaining dough together and continue to cut out doughnuts and doughnut holes.

Gently lower 4 doughnuts into the hot oil and cook, flipping once, until they're all golden brown, about 2 to 3 minutes per side. Transfer the cooked doughnuts to the wire rack and allow them to cool slightly while you fry more doughnuts. Uncover the glaze and dunk the still-hot fried doughnuts into the bowl, flipping them once or twice to ensure they are fully coated. Place the doughnuts back onto the wire rack and continue frying and glazing.

These doughnuts are best enjoyed warm from the fryer but will keep in a resealable container at room temperature for up to 3 days.

Linzer Cookies

¾ cup butter, room temperature

¾ cup sugar

2 egg yolks

1 teaspoon vanilla extract

½ teaspoon almond extract

1¼ cups all-purpose flour

¾ cup almond flour

2 teaspoons cornstarch

½ teaspoon kosher salt

¼ teaspoon baking powder

¼ teaspoon freshly grated nutmeg

Icing sugar

½ cup prepared jam

Note:

The filled cookies will become softer and cakier as they sit but they will keep in a resealable container for up to 3 days. If you prefer a firmer Linzer, store unfilled cookies in a resealable container and fill and dust with icing sugar just before serving.

Sandwich cookies are superior to all other cookies for one main reason: by eating one, you get to eat two. Think about it.

In a mixing bowl, or a stand mixer fitted with a paddle attachment, beat together the butter and sugar on high speed until light and fluffy, about 2 to 3 minutes, scraping down the bowl once or twice. Add the egg yolks and both extracts. Continue to beat just until combined, then scrape down the sides of the bowl.

In a separate bowl, whisk together both flours, cornstarch, salt, baking powder, and nutmeg. Add these dry ingredients to the butter mixture and mix on low speed just until combined.

Turn the cookie dough out onto a piece of plastic wrap and wrap well. Squish the dough into a rough 1-inch-thick disk and refrigerate for at least 1 hour, or up to 24 hours.

Line two large baking sheets with parchment paper and set aside. Unwrap the chilled cookie dough, lightly dust a work surface with icing sugar, and roll out the dough to ¼-inch thick. Using a 3- or 3½-inch round cookie cutter, cut out as many cookies as possible. Using a 1- or 1½-inch round cookie cutter, cut the centers out of half of the cookie rounds and transfer them, along with the full cookies, to the prepared baking sheets.

Gather up and reroll the dough up to three times until you have 8 full cookies and 8 windowed cookies on your baking sheets. If you reroll the dough more than three times, the resulting texture of the cookies can start to get a bit tough.

Place the baking sheets in the fridge to chill for 30 minutes. Meanwhile, preheat the oven to 350°F.

Bake the cookies, straight from the fridge, until the edges just start to turn light golden brown, 12 to 15 minutes. Allow the cookies to cool on the sheets for 10 to 15 minutes before removing to a wire rack to cool completely.

To fill, top each full cookie with 1 tablespoon of your favorite jam and spread it into an even layer. Sprinkle the windowed cookies with a dusting of icing sugar, then sandwich the cookies together.

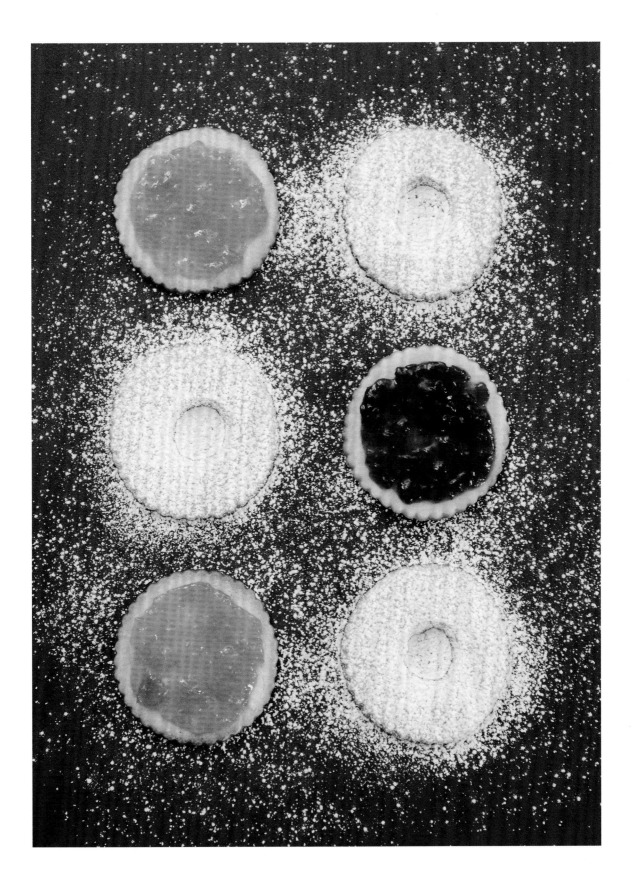

Gingerbread Whoopie Pies with Eggnog Cream

SNACKS, SIDES, SWEETS, AND SIPS · MAKES 8 PIES

FOR THE PIES

½ cup butter, room temperature

¾ cup packed brown sugar

¼ cup molasses

1 egg

2½ cups all-purpose flour

1¼ teaspoons baking soda

1 teaspoon kosher salt

2 teaspoons ground cinnamon

1 teaspoon ground ginger

½ teaspoon freshly grated nutmeg

¼ teaspoon ground allspice

1 cup buttermilk

1 teaspoon vanilla extract

FOR THE FILLING

½ cup butter, room temperature

2 cups icing sugar, plus more if needed

3–4 tablespoons eggnog

1 teaspoon vanilla extract

⅛ teaspoon freshly grated nutmeg

¼ teaspoon kosher salt

Somewhere between a cookie, a sandwich, and a cake, whoopie pies are the perfect grab-and-go sweet snack any time of the year, but this gingerbread- and eggnog-infused pie is best enjoyed after tobogganing.

Preheat your oven to 350°F and line two baking sheets with parchment paper.

For the pies, in a mixing bowl, or a stand mixer fitted with a paddle attachment, beat together the butter, sugar, and molasses on high speed until pale and fluffy, about 3 to 4 minutes. Scrape down the sides of the bowl, then add the egg and continue to beat until well combined.

In a separate bowl, whisk together the flour, baking soda, salt, cinnamon, ginger, nutmeg, and allspice. Measure out the buttermilk into a glass measuring cup and stir in the vanilla.

Mixing on low speed, add the dry ingredients to the creamed butter mixture in three additions, alternating with the buttermilk in two additions.

Using a 2 oz ice cream scoop or a ¼ cup measure, scoop eight mounds of batter about 3 inches apart onto your prepared baking sheets. Bake the cakes until they are puffed and spring back when touched, 12 to 15 minutes.

Transfer the parchment and cakes to a wire rack and allow to cool completely.

Meanwhile, make the filling by beating the butter with the icing sugar on high speed. Add 3 tablespoons of the eggnog, the vanilla, nutmeg, and salt and continue to beat until light and fluffy. If the icing feels a little thick, add about 1 tablespoon more eggnog. If it's a bit loose, add some more icing sugar.

When cool, flip half of the cakes over so they are flat side up and spread 3 to 4 tablespoons of filling onto each. Sandwich these with a plain cake and enjoy immediately or store in a resealable container at room temperature for up to 3 days.

Apricot Galette des Rois

SNACKS, SIDES, SWEETS, AND SIPS · MAKES 1 (9-INCH) GALETTE

½ cup butter, room temperature

½ cup sugar

3 eggs, divided

1 tablespoon dark rum (optional)

½ teaspoon almond extract

½ teaspoon vanilla extract

1¾ cups almond flour

¼ cup all-purpose flour

½ teaspoon kosher salt

2 sheets frozen puff pastry, thawed

¼ cup apricot jam

1 whole almond or pecan

If you live in or are visiting Quebec or France during the Christmas season, you'll find Galettes des Rois, or King Cakes, in just about every bakery window. Originally created around 300 years ago to celebrate the story of the Three Wise Men and Epiphany, a Galette des Rois is a delightfully tasty tart made of puff pastry stuffed with a frangipane filling and a bit of a surprise. Hidden among the fudgy frangipane you'll typically find a fève in the form of a dried bean or a small figurine. If you are the lucky one who finds that trinket, you get to be king for the day! In this recipe, rather than having you ask your friends to watch out for a crunchy inedible thing you've purposely hidden in your cake like a straight-up weirdo, I opt for an edible fève and use a whole almond or pecan instead.

Preheat your oven to 400°F and line a large baking sheet with parchment paper.

In a mixing bowl, or a stand mixer fitted with a paddle attachment, beat the butter and sugar on high speed until light and fluffy, about 2 to 3 minutes. Add 2 of the eggs along with the rum (if using) and both extracts and beat well to combine, about 1 minute.

In a separate bowl, whisk together both flours and the salt. Add this to the butter mixture, stirring just until combined.

Unroll 1 sheet of the pastry and, using a 9-inch cake pan as a guide, cut out a 9-inch circle and place it on the prepared baking sheet. Repeat with the other sheet of pastry but set this one aside. Place the jam in the center of the pastry on the baking sheet and spread it into an even layer, leaving about a 1-inch border all the way around. Top the jam with the almond mixture and spread that into an even layer too. The jam might get pushed out a little further into that 1-inch border but that's okay. Just try to keep as much of a border as possible. Press the whole almond into the almond mixture somewhere close to the edge, but avoid the bare border.

In a small bowl, beat the remaining egg with 2 teaspoons of water to make an egg wash. Brush the border with some egg wash and carefully drape the second pastry round over the filling, lining up the edges as much as possible. Using the sides of your hands, press and seal the edges well. For an extra-secure and decorative seal, press down the edges with a fork or, using a butter knife and two fingers, press and pinch the edges closed in a scalloped pattern.

Brush the top of the galette with the egg wash and refrigerate for 15 to 20 minutes. Once the pastry is chilled, you can use a sharp paring knife to carefully etch a pattern into the top. Whether you make a pattern or not, carefully cut five or six small vents in the top of the galette to allow steam to escape.

Bake until puffed and well browned, 35 to 40 minutes. Allow to cool completely before slicing the galette and crowning your king. Cover and store leftovers at room temperature for up to 4 days.

Cherry Cardamom Chocolate Pots

¾ cup half-and-half (10%) cream

½ cup milk

¼ teaspoon ground cardamom

2½ oz dark (around 70%) chocolate, finely chopped

3 egg yolks

3 tablespoons sugar

¼ teaspoon kosher salt

¼ teaspoon vanilla extract

¾ cup pitted sweet cherries, fresh or frozen and thawed

There is something about pudding that makes me feel ultra-indulgent and rather like a kid again. The indulgence factor is most likely due to its creaminess and the fact that, in order to enjoy it, you hardly even have to chew. The childlike wonder comes down to the fact that pudding-y desserts are always served in individual servings in my house because what is pudding without a pudding cup? These chocolate pots are a baked custard, which is essentially a more grown-up version of pudding. Slightly firmer in texture and with the added flavors of cardamom and cherry, they are the most perfectly sweet pots of pudding I could ever hope for.

Preheat your oven to 325°F and set a kettle of water to boil. Set four ¾- to 1-cup ramekins or ovenproof dishes in a 9-inch square baking dish and set aside.

Combine the cream, milk, and cardamom in a small pot and bring to a simmer over medium-low heat. Remove the pot from the heat, add the chocolate, but don't stir yet, and set aside for 2 to 3 minutes. Then, using a whisk, gently stir the mixture until the chocolate is fully melted and combined.

In a mixing bowl, whisk together the egg yolks and sugar and then whisk in the salt and vanilla. Set the bowl on a kitchen towel to stabilize it and, using one hand to continue whisking, slowly begin pouring in the hot cream and chocolate mixture until fully combined. Pass the mixture through a fine mesh sieve to strain out any curdled yolk. I like to strain it into a large measuring cup or bowl with a spout, as this helps with pouring in the next step.

Divide the cherries among the ramekins and pour the chocolate mixture over top. Carefully pour boiling water into the bottom of the square baking dish, being careful not to get any in the chocolate pots. Cover the pan tightly with aluminum foil, and bake for 40 minutes, until just set and still a little wobbly.

Take off the foil and allow the chocolate pots to cool slightly before removing them from the water. Enjoy warm, or chill, uncovered, for 2 to 3 hours in the fridge. These will keep refrigerated for up to 4 days.

Cranberry Clementine Loaf

SNACKS, SIDES, SWEETS, AND SIPS · MAKES 1 STANDARD LOAF

FOR THE LOAF

¾ cup milk

2 tablespoons + 1 teaspoon black tea leaves, divided

½ cup butter, room temperature

1 cup packed dark brown sugar

2 clementines, zested

2 eggs

1 teaspoon vanilla extract

1½ cups all-purpose flour

1 teaspoon baking powder

¼ teaspoon kosher salt

1 cup fresh or frozen cranberries

FOR THE FROSTING

½ cup brick-style cream cheese, room temperature

¼ cup butter, room temperature

1 cup icing sugar, plus more if needed

½ teaspoon vanilla extract

⅛ teaspoon ground cloves

In my humble opinion, loaves are the unsung heroes of the cake world. They don't really scream birthday or celebration, and come to think of it, they're usually only served as a quick breakfast or with a cup of tea for a mid-afternoon snack. With a flavor profile and texture falling somewhere between a muffin and a snack cake, this loaf, though, can really pack a punch. The tender crumb of the cake, the balance of sweet clementine and sour cranberry, and the creamy glaze-like frosting make for a tasty treat for any occasion.

For the loaf, in a small saucepan set over medium heat, bring the milk and 2 tablespoons of tea leaves to just under a simmer, then turn off the heat. Allow the tea to steep for 20 minutes. Strain the mixture through a fine mesh sieve, pressing out as much milk as possible from the tea leaves. Set the milk aside to cool and discard the tea leaves.

Meanwhile, preheat your oven to 350°F and grease a 5- × 9-inch loaf pan with cooking spray. Line the bottom and the long sides of the loaf pan with a sling of parchment paper and set aside.

In a mixing bowl, or a stand mixer fitted with a paddle attachment, cream together the butter, sugar, and clementine zest on high speed until light and fluffy, about 3 to 4 minutes, scraping down the bowl once or twice, as needed. Add the eggs one at a time, scraping the bowl and blending well after each addition, followed by the vanilla.

In a separate bowl, sift together the flour, baking powder, and salt. Whisk in the remaining 1 teaspoon of black tea leaves.

With the mixer running on low speed, add the dry ingredients to the butter mixture in three additions, alternating with two additions of the milk. Switch to a spatula and fold in the cranberries, mixing just until incorporated.

Transfer the batter to the prepared loaf pan and bake until a skewer inserted into the center of the loaf comes out clean, 55 to 65 minutes. Allow the loaf to cool completely in the pan.

For the frosting, in a mixing bowl, or a stand mixer fitted with a paddle attachment, beat the cream cheese and butter on high speed until smooth. Begin adding the icing sugar, ½ cup at a time, mixing on low speed between each addition and scraping down the sides of the bowl as needed. Keep adding icing sugar until your frosting is a spreadable consistency and finish by beating in the vanilla and ground cloves.

Once the loaf is cool, turn it out onto a serving dish and frost the top of the cake however you like. This loaf will keep covered in the fridge for up to 5 days.

French Lemon Tart with Macadamia White Chocolate Crust

SNACKS, SIDES, SWEETS, AND SIPS · MAKES 1 (10-INCH) TART

FOR THE CRUST

½ cup butter

¾ cup icing sugar

1 egg

½ teaspoon vanilla extract

2 cups cake and pastry flour

½ teaspoon kosher salt

3 oz white chocolate chunks

¾ cup roasted unsalted macadamia nuts

FOR THE FILLING

4 eggs

4 egg yolks

¾ cup sugar

2 tablespoons lemon zest

1 cup lemon juice

¼ teaspoon kosher salt

½ cup + 3 tablespoons butter, cut into pats

The silver lining behind dreary winter days is the fact that it is officially citrus season. In the midst of relatively slim pickings when it comes to in-season fruits, I like to view this bounty of citrus as nature's way of reminding us through food that the sun does, in fact, still exist even when we haven't had a glimpse of its rays in I don't know how long.

Preheat your oven to 350°F, lightly grease a 10-inch removable-bottom tart pan with cooking spray, and place the pan on a large baking sheet.

For the crust, in a mixing bowl, or a stand mixer fitted with a paddle attachment, beat the butter on low speed and slowly add the icing sugar until combined. Increase the speed to high and beat until light and fluffy, about 2 to 3 minutes. Scrape down the sides of the bowl and beat in the egg and vanilla until well combined, about 1 minute.

In a separate bowl, combine the flour and salt with the chocolate chunks. Roughly chop the macadamia nuts and add about one-third of them to the flour mixture. Chop the remaining nuts very finely and add them as well. Whisk well to combine.

Add the dry ingredients to the creamed butter mixture and stir just until combined. Turn the crumbly dough out into your prepared tart pan and, using your hands or the bottom of a glass, press it evenly into the bottom of the pan and up the sides. Prepare the crust for a blind bake by using a fork to poke a few dozen holes in the bottom of the crust, placing a piece of parchment paper on top, and adding pie weights or dried beans. Blind-bake the crust for 20 minutes, then remove the parchment and beans or weights and continue to bake just until set and lightly golden brown, 10 minutes.

Meanwhile, make the filling by placing a large pot containing 2 to 3 inches of water over high heat. Whisk together the eggs, yolks, sugar, lemon zest and juice, and salt in a large nonreactive heat-resistant bowl (glass or ceramic is best). Stir in the butter and place the bowl over the boiling water. Turn the heat down to low to maintain a simmer and cook, stirring frequently, until the mixture is thick and coats the back of a spoon, about 10 to 15 minutes. Remove the bowl from the heat and set aside.

When the crust is done, pour the hot filling mixture into it and place the tart in the oven until the filling is just set, 14 to 16 minutes. Allow the tart to cool completely before slicing and serving.

Note:

If you do not have a 10-inch removable-bottom tart pan, you can make this in a 9-inch cake pan or deep pie plate.

Eggnog Basque Cheesecake

SNACKS, SIDES, SWEETS, AND SIPS · MAKES 1 (10-INCH) CHEESECAKE

FOR THE CHEESECAKE

4 cups brick-style cream
cheese, room temperature

1¼ cups sugar

½ teaspoon kosher salt

¼ teaspoon freshly grated
nutmeg

6 eggs

1 cup whipping (35%) cream

1 cup eggnog

1 tablespoon dark rum

1 teaspoon vanilla extract or
½ vanilla bean, scraped

5 tablespoons all-purpose flour

FOR THE RUM WHIPPED CREAM

1 cup whipping (35%) cream

2 tablespoons icing sugar

1 tablespoon dark rum

½ teaspoon vanilla extract or
¼ vanilla bean, scraped

Freshly grated nutmeg

Note:

When cutting the cheesecake,
use a warm sharp knife and
wipe it off in between each
slice. This will ensure clean,
perfect slices.

Even though it looks and sounds fancy, Basque cheesecake is the easiest baked cheesecake out there. Rather than having you make a crust and carefully and slowly bake the cheesy custard in a finicky water bath, a Basque cheesecake is purposely baked in a hot oven under direct heat with the whole goal being to burn the heck out of it. Thanks to the eggnog, spiced rum, and nutmeg, I can't think of a more decadent and jaw-dropping wintery dessert.

Preheat your oven to 400°F and grease a 10-inch springform pan with cooking spray. Using two overlapping pieces of parchment paper, line the greased pan by pressing the parchment along the bottom of the pan and haphazardly up the sides, leaving any crinkles and folds and making sure the parchment reaches at least 2 inches above the rim of the pan. Place the pan on a baking sheet and set aside.

For the cheesecake, place the cream cheese, sugar, salt, and nutmeg in a large bowl, or a stand mixer fitted with a paddle attachment, and beat on medium speed until smooth, about 2 minutes, scraping the bowl down at least three times. Beat in the eggs one at a time, mixing well and scraping down the bowl between each addition. Add the cream, eggnog, rum, and vanilla. Mix on low speed just until combined.

Remove the bowl from its stand and sift the flour over top. Reattach the bowl and continue to beat on low speed just to incorporate, about 30 seconds, scraping down the bowl halfway through.

Pour the cheesecake mixture into the prepared pan, bake for 50 minutes, then increase the temperature to 425°F and bake until the cheesecake is deeply golden brown, 15 to 20 minutes. Allow the cheesecake to cool to room temperature before removing it from the pan and peeling away the parchment paper.

For the rum whipped cream, whip the cream, icing sugar, rum, and vanilla on medium-high speed, just until soft peaks form, about 2 to 3 minutes.

Serve the cheesecake at room temperature or chilled, topped with a dollop of rum whipped cream and a grating of fresh nutmeg. This cheesecake will keep covered in the fridge for up to 5 days.

Raspberry Mint Bellinis

SNACKS, SIDES, SWEETS, AND SIPS · MAKES 6 COCKTAILS

2 cups frozen raspberries, thawed (see note)

¼ cup icing sugar

2 tablespoons chopped mint, plus some sprigs for garnish

2 teaspoons lemon juice

1 (750 ml) bottle Prosecco, chilled

Fresh raspberries, for garnish

This is the drink I want to start my Christmas morning with. Fruity, fresh, and fizzy, the colors are perfect for the season and the raspberry mint purée makes it feel quite suitable as a breakfast beverage.

Place the raspberries along with their juices, the icing sugar, mint, and lemon juice in your blender and blend until smooth. Pass the mixture through a fine mesh sieve into a small bowl to remove the raspberry seeds and any larger bits of mint. Cover and transfer the raspberry mint purée to the fridge until ready to serve.

For the Bellini, spoon 2 to 3 tablespoons of the purée into a champagne flute and carefully top with chilled Prosecco. Give the drink a gentle stir before garnishing with 1 or 2 raspberries and a sprig of mint.

Note:

Thawed fruit tends to slump and compress, so measure the raspberries while they are still frozen to get an accurate amount.

Spiced Clementine Bourbon Sour

SNACKS, SIDES, SWEETS, AND SIPS · MAKES 2 COCKTAILS

4 oz bourbon

1½ oz clementine juice

2 oz lemon juice

¾ oz pure maple syrup

¾ oz pasteurized egg white

Ground cloves

5 sage leaves, divided

1½ cups ice cubes

Clementine segments, for garnish

Ground or whole cloves, for garnish

Sours are by far my favorite cocktail. The puckering flavor of freshly squeezed lemon juice just seems to invite sip after sip, while the winter-inspired additions of sweet clementine and spicy cloves and the drama of burning sage make this a great drink to kick off a cozy dinner for a couple or a crowd.

Add the bourbon, clementine and lemon juices, maple syrup, egg white, and a small pinch of ground cloves to a cocktail shaker and shake vigorously for 10 seconds to incorporate the egg white. Add the ice cubes to the shaker, then, using a kitchen torch or a lighter, char 3 of the sage leaves until they are smoking and hold a smolder. Immediately place the smoking sage leaves in the shaker, seal it up, and shake vigorously for 20 to 25 seconds to chill the cocktail and froth up the egg white.

Strain the cocktail into champagne coupes or lowball glasses and garnish each with a freshly charred sage leaf, a clementine segment, and some cloves.

Note:

For extra clementine flavor, rub a piece of clementine peel around the rim of each glass before pouring in the cocktail.

Cinnamon Malted White Hot Chocolate

SNACKS, SIDES, SWEETS, AND SIPS · MAKES ENOUGH MIX FOR 8 TO 10 SERVINGS

5 oz good-quality white chocolate

¾ cup malted milk powder

¾ teaspoon ground cinnamon

¼ teaspoon kosher salt

1 cup milk per serving

Marshmallows or whipped cream, and cinnamon, for serving

Malted milk powder is what I reach for when I'm looking to add a little something different to classic chocolate dishes. Perhaps it boils down to the fact that I love a malted milkshake, but the nutty sweetness it adds makes things that I often find cloyingly sweet, such as white hot chocolate, perfectly well-rounded and delicious. I'm an Ovaltine gal myself, but if you want to go with the classic and feel like a character from the BBC's adaptation of Call the Midwife, Horlicks is the way to go.

Using a Microplane or the small side of a box grater, finely grate the chocolate into a mixing bowl. Add the milk powder, cinnamon, and salt and whisk well to combine. If you're making this ahead, transfer the mix to a resealable container and keep it in the pantry for up to 6 months.

To make a serving, combine 1 cup of milk with ¼ cup of the chocolate mix in a small saucepot. Place over medium-low heat and, whisking occasionally, bring the mixture to just under a simmer. Serve immediately as-is or add marshmallows or whipped cream and a dusting of cinnamon on top.

Note:

I like to use a white chocolate bar for this recipe, my preferred choice being Green & Black's. It's got a complex, almost nutty taste that complements the malt and isn't too sweet.

Thank You!

First, to my contractually obligated roommate Aaron, thank you for excitedly sitting down to everything I've ever made, for weekend breakfasts on our kitchen floor, for all the dishes done, for always knowing what song will help me shimmy my misgivings away, and for listening to me talk aloud to myself while working on every recipe I've ever written, somehow knowing when my mutterings are rhetorical and when they require some back and forth. I've said it before and I'll say it again, you are my very favorite ex-boyfriend.

To my brilliant and zany mother, Myra "Mama B" Berg, thank you for your constant support and encouragement, your wit and love, and for allowing me to tell the world of your charming ineptitude in the kitchen that first led me to the stove. I hope the recipes in this book inspired by the food you lovingly, if begrudgingly, prepared for our family make up for that a bit. You really are a better cook than I let on.

This book baby was truly a labor of love, and I am the luckiest book mom in the world for having the opportunity to co-parent with the best of the best: Robert, Zoe, and the whole team at Appetite by Random House and Penguin Random House Canada, including the ever-amazing Michelle and Tonia.

To Robert McCullough, the best publisher I could ever dream of, your passion for food and cookbooks is endlessly inspiring, and I look forward to each and every cheers we will share with glasses of crisp Chardonnay for years and years to come.

Zoe Maslow, maker of the best book babies and human babies, thank you for being the most kind and encouraging editor, for making this whole rather daunting process an absolute treat from start to finish, and for bringing my best friend, Ruby, into this world.

To the design team, particularly Terri Nimmo, Talia Abramson, and Jen Griffiths, I can't even *deal* with how wonderful you are and how lucky I am to have such talented artists design this book. It is truly amazing how you can take hundreds of typed pages of black and white and turn them into something so perfect.

The world's largest thank-you to my partners in crime: Jenna, for lending your imaginative mind, artistic eye, and sharp taste buds to these pages, and Lauren, for capturing everything in the most beautiful light and sharing your view of the world through your photos. I don't think I can express how wonderful it is to get to work with people who are so creative, strong, and collaborative, and who also tend to fall victim to the daily work crazies at the same time as I do. I love every single day we work together and can't wait for more. Thanks for being the best book buds I could ever hope to work with.

A volley of love lasers and hugs to my brother, Michael, for being an endlessly entertaining guest at my table and for acting as inspiration for a good few recipe headers. To my new sister, Julia, for loving food and poppy seeds as much as I do. To Kyle and Renée for your fierce friendship and for coming over for dinner whenever I need a recipe tested. To Marisa for being my bulldog and for being so supportive by making almost every recipe I've ever written. To Sarah and Odie for being constant bolsters to my sometimes-wavering heart. And to Richelle and Tiffany for being my Gal Fridays, for eating too many doughnuts when I need to know which recipe tastes best, and for helping me keep my brain from turning into a bowl of oatmeal. I love you all to the Moon and back.

To the bananas bunch of humans that make up the Footes and the Kings, thank you for throwing the best parties, for making the best food, for teaching me how to *not* thaw shrimp or make Shake 'n Bake, for "bergamot" and "flan," for chapulines, and for understanding that no celebration is complete without a metric tonne of potatoes. To my Henry Island family, thank you for fostering my love of summer, for loving that island as much as I do, and for really driving home what it means to be a good neighbor. A special thank you to the Wayes, an adopted offshoot of my family, for sharing recipes, taking me fishing, and staying up late on summer nights, sharing stories about my dad. I am one of the lucky ones who gets to say things like "I have the best family in the whole world" and actually mean it.

Finally, thank you to you! Hearing from you, meeting you, and getting to see how the recipes that I love become some of your family favorites too is one of the truest pleasures in my life. I hope that, within these pages, you find recipes perfect for the ones you love and get just as much out of making and enjoying them as I did writing them.

Thank you for continuing to have me at your table!

Index